An Introduction to the Life and Works of
Laurence Sterne

Published by The Langley Press, 2020

To Christopher Willmot

An Introduction to the Life and Works of
Laurence Sterne

Simon Webb

Also from the Langley Press

Where Did Shakespeare Get His Ideas?
The Sources of Shakespeare's Plays: An Introduction
Macbeth (With Zombies)
Aaron of Lincoln
Nicholas Breakspear: The Pope from England
Adeland of Bath: Twelfth Century Renaissance Man
The Life and Legend of Nicholas Flamel: Discoverer of the
Philosopher's Stone?

For free downloads and more from the Langley Press, please
visit our website at http://tinyurl.com/lpdirect

Contents

Bust of Sterne by Nollekens (NY Metropolitan Museum)

I. Burials and Births

Some time during the latter part of March 1768, a long, thin human corpse was extracted by grave-robbers from a burial ground near Tyburn in London. Somehow the body was transported to Cambridge, where it made an appearance at a class run by the university's professor of anatomy, Charles Collignon. Collignon, a published author and noted musical composer (or someone else who was in attendance) recognised the distinctive face of the corpse, although by now the body would have been stripped and shaved all over. It turned out that the anatomists were about to dissect the body of the Rev. Laurence Sterne, author of *Tristram Shandy* and *A Sentimental Journey*, who had died in his London lodgings on the eighteenth of March.

Literary lions, Anglican priests and people who had managed to combine the two roles were not supposed to be made available for dissection in eighteenth-century England. The law provided for the bodies of a few executed convicts to serve in this way, but the medical schools' appetite for fresh subjects could not be satisfied by that meagre provision. Demand outstripped supply, and the slack was taken up by the notorious resurrectionists or grave-robbers. Collignon, himself a remarkably skinny man, is said to have decided that the dissection of Laurence Sterne should proceed. The medics now had free access to the body which had once contained what both Nietzsche and Goethe described as one of the most liberated spirits that ever existed.

The story of the afterlife of Sterne's body comes from various sources and is not entirely reliable. It is thought that, after the dissection, Collignon ordered his subject to be returned to the graveyard near Tyburn, which belonged to St George's Church, Hanover Square. When this area was scheduled for re-development in the 1960s, Sterne enthusiast Kenneth Monkman, founder of the Laurence Sterne Trust, arranged for several likely skulls to be examined in the hope that that of the author might be identified. By comparing one skull to the marble bust of Sterne made by the sculptor Joseph Nollekens in 1766, it was determined that it was indeed that of Laurence Sterne. The fact that there were cut-marks, as from anatomists' scalpels, on the skull added further weight to the final choice.

The skull, together with some bones found near it, was re-buried in the graveyard of St Michael's Church, Coxwold, the parish church of the Yorkshire village where Sterne was vicar from 1760 until his death. Today these remains lie under a stone made to resemble the black page that appeared near the end of the twelfth chapter of volume one of Sterne's novel *Tristram Shandy*.

The prospect of dissection after death was supposed to strike terror into the hearts of English Christians in the eighteenth century. Many believed fervently in the doctrine of the Resurrection of the Body at the Day of Judgement, and were concerned about how they would rise again to greet Jesus if, for instance, their brains had been taken out of their skulls. The resurrectionists worked in a legal grey area, since the bodies they stole did not really belong to anyone, but they sometimes had to face violence from indignant friends and relatives of the pilfered dead.

Whatever his opinion about the words concerning the Resurrection of the Body in the Christian creeds, Sterne was certainly aware of the possibility of his own dissection after death, as was his contemporary, the artist William Hogarth. Hogarth depicted a crowded anatomy lab in his terrifying picture *The Reward of Cruelty*. Here, three different men with knives are slicing the body of a convict, who still has part of the hangman's noose around his neck. A pompous professor is probing the body with a long stick, while a fifth man is pulling the cadaver's entrails into a barrel.

In *Tristram Shandy*, Sterne, in the voice of his narrator, the eponymous Tristram, writes about *when* he will be dissected, and not *if*:

whenever my brains come to be dissected, you will perceive, without spectacles, that [my father] has left a large uneven thread, as you sometimes see in an unsaleable piece of cambrick, running along the whole length of the web

(*Tristram Shandy*, Book VI, Chapter XXXIII)

Sterne also hints at what will be discovered inside the bodies of men who, in life, did not appreciate what Tristram calls the 'delicious mixture' to be discerned in women's characters:

he who hates [women] for it - all I can say of the matter is - That he has either a pumpkin for his head - or a pippin for his heart, -and whenever he is dissected 'twill be found so

(*TS*, Book V, Chapter IX)

Here a very lightweight comic idea – about a man having a pumpkin instead of a brain – is suddenly turned dark in the last words of the passage. This is a very typical stylistic twist from Sterne. Likewise, a diverting passage on the scientific study of noses brings us up short with:

Prignitz . . . who with infinite learning, and from the most candid and scholar-like examination of above four thousand different skulls, in upwards of twenty charnel-houses in Silesia . . .

(*TS*, III, XXXVIII)

9

Tristram Shandy himself is a mouthpiece for Sterne, but, as we shall see, in many respects the author more closely resembles the character of Parson Yorick in his *Tristram Shandy*. The medieval Danish jester Sterne claims as his cleric's ancestor appears only as a skull recently dug out of a grave in Shakespeare's *Hamlet*. The practice of re-using graves was a way for corpses to be disturbed without the involvement of any anatomists. Readers of *Hamlet* should note that Yorick was buried well within living memory, yet Shakespeare shows him being dug up again.

While parts of Laurence Sterne sleep at Coxwold, we must assume that the whole of his great-grandfather Archbishop Richard Sterne lies in York Minster, which boasts a fine memorial to this earlier Sterne, carved by Grinling Gibbons. Richard seems to have come from fairly humble origins in Mansfield, Nottinghamshire. He attended the free school there, and was a sizar at Trinity College, Cambridge: this means that he had to 'work his passage' through part of his time at university, acting as a paid servant while pursuing his studies.

Richard Sterne distinguished himself as a scholar and became master of Jesus College, Cambridge in 1634. By this time he was probably already chaplain to William Laud, then Archbishop of Canterbury. Four years later he was a royal chaplain, but soon Richard's rise was interrupted by the growing power of the Puritans and the beginning of the Civil Wars in Britain.

In August 1642 Laurence Sterne's great-grandfather was arrested for attempting to transfer large quantities of college plate to the king, and was imprisoned for a time in London: his imprisonment included ten days locked in the hold of a coal ship on the Thames. Stripped of his various preferments, benefices, offices and other sources of income, he later supported himself and his wife Elizabeth by keeping a school at Stevenage in Hertfordshire. After the Restoration of Charles II, Richard Sterne's (interrupted) rise resumed. In 1660 he became Bishop of Carlisle, and in 1664 Archbishop of York. In the Church of England, there are only ever two archbishops, and two corresponding provinces or sets of dioceses; those belonging to Canterbury and York. Among the Archbishop's thirteen children by his wife Elizabeth was Simon Sterne, named after Richard's father, who became the grandfather of Laurence Sterne.

Archbishop Richard Sterne established the wealth and status of his branch of the Sterne family tree, but by English tradition the wealth could not be enjoyed by all of his descendants. As usual, the eldest son took the lion's share of the inheritance, while daughters and younger sons had to shift for themselves. Simon Sterne, the grandfather of the novelist, was the Archbishop's second son, but he secured his fortune by marrying Mary Jaques, a Yorkshire heiress. Laurence Sterne's father Roger was the second son of Simon, but he was not so fortunate in his own marriage: in 1711 he wed Agnes Nuttall, the daughter of a sutler or supplier to the army. In his brief *Memoirs*, Sterne himself adds that his father owed Agnes's father money. By this time, Roger was an ensign in the army: Laurence Sterne was born at Clonmel in County Tipperary, Ireland, on the twenty-fourth of November 1713, while his father was posted there.

According to Stephen Gwynne's *History of Ireland*, large numbers of British troops were posted in Ireland during the eighteenth century, not just to keep the native population in check and guarantee the continued safety and vast privileges of the Protestant British oligarchy. The British wanted to maintain a large standing army, but the cost of keeping too many soldiers in England tended to raise objections from the English themselves. Much better to keep hundreds of troops in Ireland, where the locals had been mercilessly ground down by the British for decades and were in no position to complain.

Sterne was not the only great eighteenth-century comic writer of English to be born in Ireland. His contemporaries Oliver Goldsmith and Jonathan Swift were both born there, and, like Sterne, Swift also became an Anglican clergyman (Goldsmith was the son of a clergyman). Although as Dean of St Patrick's Anglican Cathedral in Dublin Swift was part of the Protestant hierarchy in Ireland, he wrote pieces like *A Modest Proposal* (1729) to shed light on how the native Irish were being treated. Drawing on a type of dark humour familiar to readers of Sterne, Swift suggests, in *A*

Modest Proposal, that the poor of Ireland should be allowed to profit by raising their children to be eaten by their better-off contemporaries.

As recorded in Douglas Hyde's *Literary History of Ireland*, the native poets who still wrote in Irish were even more direct than Swift about their treatment at the hands of the British:

Under frost, under snow, under rain, under blasts of wind, without a morsel to eat but watercress, green grass, sorrel of the mountain, or clover of the hills. Och! My pity to see their nobles forsaken.

Their estates are estimated for, and are now in the hands of robbers, their towns are under the control of English-speaking bastards . . .

An earlier poem in a similar vein translated by Hyde complains how after 'every conceivable treachery' the English 'cheese-eating clowns' transported numbers of the Irish 'to the country of Jamaica'.

II. Childhood, Cambridge and the Church

In his *Memoir*, written for his daughter Lydia, Sterne describes his father as:

> a little smart man — active to the last degree, in all exercises — most patient of fatigue and disappointments, of which it pleased God to give him full measure — he was in his temper somewhat rapid, and hasty — but of a kindly, sweet disposition, void of all design; and so innocent in his own intentions, that he suspected no one; so that you might have cheated him ten times in a day, if nine had not been sufficient for your purpose

Here Sterne is not using the word 'smart' in the American sense of 'intelligent': as a soldier, Ensign Roger Sterne would have been expected to be smart in the sense of tidy in his clothes and person. Laurence's description of his father suggests that he may not have had much in the way of 'smarts' in the American sense at all. This might help to explain why he did not rise to any great rank in the army, although he came from an impressive family, descended from an archbishop. As Ian Campbell Ross points out in his biography of Sterne, in those days Roger would have had to pay to buy a promotion, but saving up or otherwise acquiring the money to do this would also have required 'smarts'.

Sterne claimed that on the day after he, Laurence, was born, his father's regiment was broken up, and Roger found himself without employment and with a wife and two children to support. The other child was Laurence's elder sister Mary, 'born in Lisle in

French Flanders' in 1712. Threatened with penury and homelessness, the Sternes beat a retreat to Roger's mother's house at Elvington, near York. By this time, Laurence's grandfather Simon had been dead for ten years. From the rest of Sterne's *Memoir*, it would seem that though, as a younger son, Roger may not have derived any regular income from the Sterne family fortune, he was often able to find shelter in the scattered homes of his better-off relatives.

After about ten months at Elvington, the family was called back to the regiment at Dublin, and there then followed too many years when Roger was posted for a short time to a variety of different places. Sometimes his family went with him, at other times they were forced to follow when they were able. As a boy, Sterne therefore gained some fleeting experience of Exeter, the Isle of Wight, and Dublin, Wicklow, Carrickfergus, Drogheda, Mullengar, Londonderry and Annamoe in Ireland. During this time Sterne acquired new siblings, some of whom, like the oddly-named Joram and Devijeher, died as children. In this constantly-shifting life, there were 'many perils, and struggles', and on more than one occasion the family was nearly lost at sea.

At Annamoe in Ireland, Sterne fell into a mill-race while it was running – a consequence, perhaps, of the old-fashioned habit of letting small children roam around unsupervised. Amazingly, the future novelist was 'taken up unhurt' after this adventure, and 'hundreds of the common people' flocked to see him, as his escape seemed miraculous.

In his book on the English humorists of the eighteenth century, the novelist William Makespeace Thackeray paints a rosy picture of Sterne's life as a child following the regiment. Laurence, says Thackeray, 'had lived with the followers of William [III] and Marlborough, and had beat time with his little feet to the fifes of Ramillies in Dublin barrack-yard'. Sterne's own reminiscences do not, however, look back fondly on childhood hours spent playing 'with the torn flags and halberds of Malplaquet on the parade-ground at Clonmel'.

At the age of ten Laurence was sent to live with his uncle Richard, his father's older brother, at Woodhouse in Yorkshire. He attended school at nearby Hipperholme, and in term-time may have lived at the school, where he was 'severely whipped' by the usher for writing his name on the school-room ceiling while it was being re-painted. By contrast, Sterne's actual school-master, the Rev. Nathan Sharpe, suggested that the 'tag' should never be effaced, because Sterne 'was a boy of genius, and he was sure I should come to preferment'.

Sterne's road to preferment took him to Jesus College Cambridge in 1733, at the age of twenty. By now both his father and his uncle Richard had died, the former in 1731 in Jamaica at about the age of forty. Sterne tells us that Roger had got into a 'quarrel begun about a goose' while stationed on Gibraltar, and had been 'run through the body by Captain Phillips, in a duel'. Sterne's father survived for a while, but after he was posted to Jamaica his weakened constitution meant that he could not survive 'the country fever' of that island.

Luckily for Laurence, his cousin Richard, his late uncle Richard's son and namesake, decided to support him through his years at Jesus College. This was, of course, the college where the great-grandfather they shared had been master both before and after the Interregnum. Like that celebrated great-grandfather, Laurence Sterne began as a sizar.

Despite the presence of the future author of *Tristram Shandy*, Cambridge, it seems, was not a particularly stimulating place to be a student in the 1730s. Both teaching and learning were at a low ebb, as were the numbers of students. Scholars from wealthier families regarded their college years as a sort of extended holiday, and many did not even bother to take a degree. Unlike Sterne, there was no necessity for them to become qualified to enter a profession, as they knew their lives would consist of living off private incomes in fine houses in the country and/or in town. Some, including Jonathan Swift, felt that many students at both Oxford and Cambridge learned little more than how to drink, and smoke tobacco.

Living, as he was at first, on a small allowance from his cousin Richard, Sterne was probably unable to participate in many of the more outré high jinks of his wealthier fellow-students, but at least his time at Jesus College was enlivened by a close friendship with John Hall, who was to remain a life-long friend of the author. Hall changed his name to Hall-Stevenson when he married a Yorkshire heiress in 1740; Sterne, who was by then a Church of England priest, officiated at the wedding. Miss Anne Stevenson came with a fortune of twenty-five thousand pounds, worth over three million today, but as the son of a successful Durham lawyer Hall was not exactly hard-up before he became Hall-Stevenson. He left college about 1738, without taking a degree, and went on the Grand Tour.

Sterne's friendship with Hall was based on a mutual interest in certain types of literature, some of it French and decidedly disreputable. Among their favourite authors was François Rabelais, a sixteenth-century French monk whose works still seem breathtakingly uninhibited. According to a memoir of Sterne that has been attributed to Hall-Stevenson, it was 'his Rabelaisian spirit' that led his old college friend to write *Tristram Shandy*. Hall-Stevenson himself published bawdy tales and verses from about the middle of the century, many of which were inspired by and/or referred to Sterne's own books. Despite his marriage, Hall-Stevenson put himself at the centre of what used to be called 'a fast set' which got up to all sorts of mischief at Skelton Castle in Yorkshire, which Hall-Stevenson's father had bought from his own father-in-law.

In Hall-Stevenson Sterne acquired a life-long friend, although perhaps not the kind of friend who was suitable for a future priest of the Church of England. At Cambridge he also acquired a life-long enemy, in the form of tuberculosis, known as 'consumption' in those days, because of its tendency to cause sufferers to lose their appetites and become sometimes painfully thin. There was no cure for TB in the eighteenth century, and even today many cases resist the most up-to-date treatment. Some eighteenth-century patients managed to keep their symptoms at bay, but for many, a diagnosis meant a shortened life punctuated by recurring bouts of illness, with one last episode that carried them off – as happened to Sterne.

Those who could afford it, as Sterne could later in life, roamed around looking for a cure, or alleviation of their symptoms, or a climate that would make them less liable to relapses. Tourism, in parts of the south of France and Switzerland in particular, began when large numbers of wealthy sufferers began to arrive in search of better air. In England, spa towns like Bath cashed in on the supposedly beneficial effects of their water.

As we have seen, Sterne's school and college educations were funded and presided over first by his uncle Richard and then by his cousin Richard. Even with a Cambridge degree and his ordination as a priest, Sterne could easily have spent his entire career as a poor curate in an obscure village somewhere. Many worthy men did, and, as Sterne's contemporary at Cambridge Thomas Gray wrote of most of humanity, they found that they were flowers 'born to blush unseen' who wasted their 'sweetness on the desert air'.

For many young clergymen, the key to the kind of preferment predicted for Sterne by his old schoolmaster the Rev. Nathan Sharpe was help from powerful friends and relatives. Thanks to the influence of his uncle Dr Jaques Sterne, a younger brother of his father Roger, Laurence was able to enjoy considerable preferment – but at a price.

One assumes that twenty-first century twenty-somethings who opt for a career as priests in the Church of England are motivated by an exceptional level of Christian devotion, are already deeply involved in at least one local Anglican church, and have probably lived (or plan to live) celibate lives until they marry. We cannot assume that any of this was true of Laurence Sterne when he decided to take holy orders. Sterne did not have the wide choice of careers open to him that university graduates have today. His tuberculosis and his exceptionally light-boned build would have excluded him from the army or navy, and in any case he probably felt that as a child he had already seen enough of army life. Both the armed services and the law would have required the payment of large premiums before Sterne could have started on a firm footing, and Sterne's family and social circle would have regarded trade as beneath them. A good start in trade also required the payment of very high fees to gain access, a hurdle that must have been successfully cleared by Sterne's fictional creation, Walter Shandy.

Exceptional religious devotion, such as must inspire many modern candidates for the ministry, would in any case have been regarded with suspicion by the typical eighteenth-century Anglican churchman, if Laurence Sterne had displayed any. It was this kind of fanaticism that had fuelled the Civil Wars and the Interregnum of the previous century, which had seen Sterne's great-grandfather locked up and threatened with execution. As we shall see, Sterne showed an awareness of this dire historical precedent in his sermons.

A clergymen who took the moral teachings of Jesus Christ seriously might also have objected to the horrendous corruption of the Church of England in Sterne's day, which saw men from wealthy, powerful families acquiring even more wealth and power, while actual service to the Church and its congregations, and the support of poor clergymen and their families, were woefully neglected.

III. Yorkshire

Jaques Sterne, who had a good, and then a bad, influence on his nephew Laurence's career in the Church, had been given his mother's maiden surname as a Christian name. Like Laurence, he had attended Jesus College, Cambridge, and by the time Laurence was absorbed into his circle, he had benefited from so much preferment in the church that he was earning over nine hundred pounds a year – worth over one hundred thousand today. He was based at York, where he lived in some style and was recognised as one of the city's movers and shakers.

Jaques had taken full advantage of the deeply corrupt system of the time, whereby clergymen could acquire the incomes from various livings, prebends and offices (meaning ecclesiastical jobs) without being expected to do much if any of the work these jobs required. The holders of these offices – who were called 'pluralists' - would condescend to pay a little out of their fortunes to employ poor, hard-working curates and other substitutes to do the work they themselves should have been doing.

In 1738, Jaques secured for Laurence Sterne the living of Sutton-on-the Forest, just a few miles north of the city of York. Unlike many of his clerical contemporaries, Jaques' nephew had not had to languish for years as a curate – he got Sutton just a week after his ordination. He was not, however, allowed to spend all his time as a country vicar: his uncle Jaques required his presence in York to assist in his political schemes. In classic eighteenth-century style, Laurence paid a curate to do much of his work at Sutton, and early in 1741 he became prebendary of Givendale, meaning that, probably with little extra work, he was able to benefit from the income York Minster derived from the Yorkshire hamlet of that name.

Although the air may have been worse for his lungs than the air at Sutton, aspects of life in York at this time may have appealed to Sterne more than the life of a country vicar. The city had coffee-houses, assembly-rooms, concerts and theatricals, and even its own newspapers. Many English cities have been so enthusiastically redeveloped since the Second World War that a time-traveller from the 1740s would struggle to recognise them. Not so York: thanks to a kind of benign neglect it has retained the old pattern of many of its streets, and a number of very old buildings, especially around the Minster. The twenty-first century visitor can therefore get a pretty good idea of what York was like when Laurence Sterne lived there.

Among York sights that Sterne pilgrims should certainly visit is the so-called Treasurer's House in Minster Yard, parts of which date back to the sixteenth century. Sterne's uncle Jaques lived in the north wing of this house, which he bought in 1742 and refurbished in sumptuous style.

Shortly after his installation as a prebendary, Sterne married Elizabeth Lumley, a young lady of York, whom he claimed he had been courting for two years. It would have been grossly irresponsible for him as a TB sufferer to have married a healthy woman, as he would almost certainly have passed the infection to her. The moral alternatives were, to remain a bachelor, or marry a fellow-sufferer. Sterne chose the second option, and it is to be hoped that the mysterious Miss C, who rejected Sterne's advances at around this time, was also infected.

Elizabeth was a genteel orphan, living on a small private income with just one servant in Little Alice Lane, near York Minster. Sterne's description, from the memoir he wrote for their daughter Lydia, of the moment their relationship finally tipped over into a decision to marry, is romantic, but also deeply melancholy:

at York I become acquainted with your mother, and courted her for two years — she owned she liked me, but thought herself not rich enough, or me too poor, to be joined together — she went to her sister's in S — , and I wrote to her often — I believe then she was partly determined to have me, but would not say so — at her return she fell into a consumption — and one evening that I was sitting by her with an almost broken heart to see her so ill, she said, "my dear Lawrey, I can never be yours, for I verily believe I have not long to live — but I have left you every shilling of my fortune;" — upon that she shewed me her will — this generosity overpowered me. — It pleased God that she recovered, and I married her in the year 1741.

In his *Memoir*, Sterne follows his description of this affecting scene with an account of his getting the prebendary of Givendale, and then more about his uncle Jaques, the 'party man' who employed him to 'write paragraphs in the newspapers'.

Laurence Sterne's career as a political journalist was concentrated in the period covering the York by-election of 1741. There had already been a parliamentary election that year, but the process had to be repeated because one of Yorkshire's two county MPs, the Tory Charles Howard, Viscount Morpeth, died of consumption (Sterne's own disease) on the ninth of August. As often happened in England at that time, Charles had not had to contend with a rival candidate, and had been returned unopposed. This had happened because the rival party – the Whigs – had not had time to find someone to stand against him. Now that the Viscount's death offered them a second chance, the York Whigs in general, and Jaques Sterne in particular, were determined to make a fight of it.

The city of York was very much split along party lines. Even the York County Infirmary, recently founded by Dr John Burton, of whom more later, was seen as a Tory institution, and as such was criticised by the Whigs. In March 1741 Archdeacon Jaques Sterne had been instrumental in founding a local Whig newspaper, the *York Gazetteer*, to counter the Tory *York Courant*; but just before the new paper launched, its printer, John Jackson, had been assaulted by a Tory yobbo called John Garbutt. Garbutt's character and the circumstances surrounding the assault were included among the matters discussed in the rival York newspapers and elsewhere as the by-election gained momentum.

During the election campaign, poems, letters and articles, some of them notably bitter and intemperate, appeared in print, and at one point Sterne gave in to the temptation to compare one of his opponents to 'a certain nasty animal in Egypt' that was said to spray shit on its enemies. Since some controversial pieces were unsigned, or marked only by the author's initials, there was a great deal of confusion about who had written what, and some unfounded accusations were made. There was also a sense that clergymen like Sterne should not be involved in such work. Not surprisingly, Sterne later wrote in his *Memoir* that he found this business of writing 'paragraphs in the newspapers' 'dirty work' that was 'beneath me'. The York county by-election did, however, see Sterne's writings printed and read for the first time, and not just in Yorkshire.

After his controversial participation in the York by-election of 1741, Sterne retired with his new wife to his vicarage at Sutton-in-the-Forest, resumed the life of a country vicar and dispensed with the services of the curate he had hired to cover the work while he was fighting in the political trenches at York. He planted cherries, apples, nectarines and peaches in the garden, installed sash windows, fitted new ceilings, installed a new fire-place in the parlour and had a great deal of plaster and stucco applied.

From these details of the interior work recorded in his parish book, it would seem that Sterne was paying to convert the old vicarage into something like a fashionable eighteenth-century house, such as both Laurence and Elizabeth would have seen at York. As we shall see, a sash window was to play an important role in Sterne's future masterpiece *Tristram Shandy*. Tristram's father is also so obsessed with the fruit that he grows in his walled garden that he is very upset when he has to be away from home during the days when some of it is due to ripen (*TS* I, XVI).

It seems that even with his income from the prebendary of North Newbald (which he had swapped with that of Givendale), his wife's private income, and the living of Sutton, Sterne could not make ends meet. The cost of 'civilising' the house and bringing it into the eighteenth century was just one example of how the Sternes tended to live beyond their means. The financial situation was still tight after Laurence had acquired the additional living of Stillington. This had not reached him due to any help from his now-estranged uncle Jaques, but as a consequence of his marriage. Elizabeth had inherited the living, but as a woman (who could not take holy orders) only a future husband of Elizabeth's could benefit by it, if he happened to be a clergyman.

The young couple's troubles went beyond concerns about their finances. In those days, the life of a country parson could be greatly improved if he enjoyed a good relationship with the local landowner. At Sutton, the Sternes were not 'upon a very friendly footing' with 'the 'Squire of the parish', Philip Harland. Harland was a Tory, and it seems that he had preferred the company of Richard Wilkinson, the curate Sterne had had to dismiss on his return to permanent residence at Sutton-in-the-Forest.

The Sternes were on better terms with the Harlands' equivalents at Stillington, the Croft family, of whom Sterne writes in his *Memoir* that they 'shewed us every kindness— 'twas most truly agreeable to be within a mile and a half of an amiable family, who were ever cordial friends'. The Crofts' retrospective impressions of the Sternes are recorded in the form of anecdotes in a book called *The Whitefoord Papers*, 'being the correspondence and other manuscripts of Colonel Charles Whitefoord and Caleb Whitefoord from 1739 to 1810'. The 'other manuscripts' include letters containing anecdotes about the Sternes sent to Caleb Whitefoord by John Croft. Although Sterne praised the Crofts' kindness, John does not write very kindly about Sterne, and his anecdotes about the writer hint at serious problems at the Sutton parsonage.

According to Croft, Sterne fell out with his uncle Jaques over a woman who was a mistress of his uncle, but was made pregnant by Laurence himself. The child lived into adulthood, and was a lady who was 'said to resemble Sterne very much'. It is not clear whether this lady is supposed to have been conceived before Sterne's engagement to Elizabeth Lumley, but Croft assures us that Sterne's wife was 'a homely woman'. Whenever Sterne's affair with Jaques' mistress is supposed to have happened, Croft tells us that Sterne's 'infidelity to the marriage bed' wrecked the Sternes' relationship. On one occasion, Elizabeth felt obliged to literally drag Sterne off one of their maids, an experience, Croft tells us, that drove the unfortunate Mrs Stern 'out of her senses'.

There is evidence to suggest that the pressures of life with such an unreliable spouse did indeed drive Elizabeth Sterne out of her senses and, in her case, into a delusion that she was the Queen of Bohemia. The delusion, or some other form of illness, probably psychiatric in nature, may have maintained its hold on Elizabeth all through the time when Laurence was writing the first two volumes of *Tristram Shandy*. As Sterne told his friend the Marquis of Buckingham, 'it was every word of it wrote in affliction; & under a constant uneasiness of mind'.

John Croft also tells us about another type of infidelity which characterised Sterne's behaviour as a parish priest. On his way to preach at Stillington one Sunday morning, Laurence spotted some partridges. He immediately went home and got his gun 'and left his Flock that was waiting for him in the Church, in the lurch'. Croft also gives us a neat summary of the Sternes' attempt to make money from farming, on local land they had bought for the purpose:

They kept a Dairy Farm at Sutton, had seven milch cows, but they always sold their Butter cheaper than their Neighbours, as they had not the least idea of economy, [so] that they were always behindhand and in arrears with Fortune

According to Croft, Sterne's parishioners 'generally considered him as crazy, or crackbrained' and were so 'at variance' with him that none of them tried to rescue him when he fell into deep water through some ice at Stillington.

It may be that their neighbours would have looked more kindly on the Sternes if they had produced a large brood of adorable children to fill the parsonage. In fact, after still-births and infant mortality had taken their toll, the Sternes only ever produced one child who lived into adulthood – the aforementioned Lydia, born in 1747.

In *The Whitefoord Papers*, John Croft also asserts that Sterne was such a poor preacher that when it was his turn to give a sermon at York Minster 'half of the congregation usually went out of church as soon as he mounted the pulpit, as his delivery and voice were so very disagreeable'. Other evidence suggests that Sterne was in fact an excellent preacher, and was generally more valuable to his flock and his diocese than Croft's tales would suggest; but unsettling gossip, particularly about Sterne's infidelities, has also been preserved in other sources. *New Light on Sterne*, edited by James M Kuist and published in 1965, includes information on Sterne from his one-time servant, Richard Greenwood. Unlike Croft, Greenwood judged his old master to have been a good preacher, but he also recalled that whenever he visited York, 'he rarely spent the night without a girl or two'.

IV. A Political Romance and the Rabelaisian Fragment

In his *Memoir*, Sterne told his daughter that he 'remained near twenty years at Sutton' and Stillington, 'doing duty at both places – I had then very good health. Books, painting, fiddling, and shooting were my amusements'. No writings of any significance from this period have been identified as Sterne's, and the fact that his party-political writings during the 1741 by-election at York are also comparatively insignificant puts the vicar of Sutton and Stillington into the class of writers who only met with literary fame late in life. In the twentieth century, such writers included Proust, Toni Morrison, Henry Miller, Tolkien and the Portuguese writer José Saramago. Apart from Saramago, all of these were in their forties when they first started to attract serious attention as authors. Saramago was in his sixties. Laurence Sterne was forty-six in 1759 when *Tristram Shandy* began to fly off the bookshop shelves in London. In the same year, his *Political Romance* had met with a less enthusiastic reception at York.

Like the 'paragraphs in the newspapers' that Sterne had written during the York by-election of 1741, the *Political Romance* is an occasional piece, inspired by local events in which Sterne himself was involved, though on the periphery. The events centred on Dr Francis Topham, a leading ecclesiastical lawyer based in York, who was born in the same year as Sterne, and was also a Cambridge graduate. The whole business was very complex: the following is an outline.

It was felt locally that Topham spent rather too much of his time pushing for more of the kinds of preferments and lucrative

Church offices from which Sterne himself had benefited. In 1751 Topham became 'commissary and keeper-general of the exchequer and prerogative court of the archbishop' of York, a very impressive piece of preferment, which did not, however, satisfy his ambition. He angled for the 'commissaryship of the peculiar court of Pickering and Pocklington', but was disappointed when this was awarded to one Laurence Sterne.

Things came to a head in 1758 when Topham discovered that the aforementioned job of 'commissary and keeper-general of the exchequer and prerogative court of the archbishop' of York was one that used to be awarded to new holders of the office in such a way that they could, in effect, leave the position as a bequest to a suitable person. Topham wanted his son Edward to inherit the role: Archbishop Gilbert wanted to agree to Topham's plan, out of gratitude for his many services, but said he had to pass the proposal to the Dean and Chapter. The idea was rejected, although Topham had already had the relevant legal documents drawn up, ready for the Dean's seal.

This sent Topham into a towering rage: his rage became particularly evident when he fell out with Dean Fountayne at a York dinner that was also attended by Sterne. Sterne repaired to his writing-desk to pen a satire on the whole affair. The result was *A Political Romance*, otherwise known as *The History of a Good Warm Watch-Coat*, published in 1759.

Sterne attempted to ridicule Topham's discomfiture by telling a ludicrous fictional story similar to that of Topham's various attempts to secure career advantages. The setting of the *Romance* is not, however, the higher echelons of the Church in York, but a simple country parish. The Archbishop is replaced by a humble parson, Topham himself by Trim, the sexton and dog-whipper for the parish, 'a little, dirty, pimping, pettifogging, ambidextrous Fellow, — who neither cared what he did or said of any, provided he could get a Penny by it'. The commissaryship is represented by a watch-coat, i.e. a coat of a type designed to be worn on watch during very cold weather.

Trim asks the parson if he can take the old coat and divide it up to be fashioned into new garments for himself and his wife. Like

Archbishop Gilbert, the parson says he must refer the question to others, but soon Trim reappears with the coat already split in two. The parish-clerk (meaning the Dean) and various parish officials object to Trim's premature action, and reject his long-winded defence of it, deciding 'that Trim, in every Part of this Affair, had behaved very ill'. In response, Trim 'huff'd and bounced most terribly', 'raise[d] an uproar in the Town' and reminded everybody of earlier injustices that had been perpetrated against him. At last, Trim is humiliated by a mob in the town-square, where he cannot defend his greediness and overweening ambition.

Sterne himself appears in *A Political Romance*, in the guise of 'Lory Slim'; the commissaryship Sterne gained against Topham's wishes is represented by a pair of second-hand breeches inherited by Lory from the Parish Clerk.

Although the characters who feature in the main body of the *Political Romance* are satirical stand-ins for Topham, Archbishop Gilbert, Dean Fountayne, Sterne himself and others, they are effective as characters in themselves. The odious Trim, a combination of busybody, barrack-room lawyer, malcontent and toady, is quite believable, and may have been based on a character or characters with whom Sterne had dealings in his country parishes. The author's experiences of society in York are reflected in the so-called 'key' to the *Romance*, which is an account of an impromptu discussion about the book conducted by the members of a political club held in the city.

Various members of the club propose that the *Romance*, which is supposed to have been found dropped by accident in the Minster-Yard, is a satire on Continental politics, or on the Church in general, or the law, or the medical profession, or a recent election. None hit on the right interpretation; but Sterne's meaning was all too clear to the real-life churchmen who read *A Political Romance* when it was first published in 1759. It was felt to show the Church of England at York, and indeed elsewhere, in a very bad light, and an official of the Minster was sent round all the local bookshops to buy up as many copies as possible: these were then burned. A mangled version of the *Romance* was published in 1769, but the full, correct version as originally printed did not come to light until 1905.

It is tempting to spot signs of Sterne 'limbering up' for the task of writing *Tristram Shandy*, in his *Political Romance*. There is a comical chaos about events in Trim's parish which is reminiscent of the chaotic atmosphere of Shandy Hall in *Tristram*, and Trim's general busyness is reminiscent of the constant activity of his namesake Corporal Trim in the later novel. The difference is that where the Trim of the *Romance* is motivated by self-interest, Corporal Trim is spurred on to new efforts by his love for uncle Toby.

Though it is quite short, the narrative structure of the *Romance* is complex, because Sterne obliges himself to repeatedly break into the main narrative to give the 'back story' that explains the main story. The 'back story' of the watch-coat involves various elements, including the aforementioned second-hand breeches, a table and various church ornaments. The comical use of explanatory digressions is also an important feature of *Tristram*.

There is a certain amount of intellectual snobbery to be seen in Sterne's 'key' to *A Political Romance*, with its political club vainly attempting to interpret the manuscript that has accidentally fallen into their hands. The members include an alderman, an apothecary, a man-midwife, a parson and a tailor, and there is a sense that if the general level of education among them had been a little higher, they might have interpreted the *Romance* more correctly. They use made-up words like 'adulterydom' and 'ichnography', and seem unable to listen to others' opinions, while sometimes stating their own with undue confidence.

There are signs that the members of the political club are obsessed with certain hobby-horses, the hobby-horse being an animal that is often to be met with in the pages of *Tristram Shandy*. The tailor, for instance, immediately seizes on the mention of the breeches in the story, and tries to make out that they symbolise the island of Sicily.

The way that the political club debates the *Romance* is reminiscent of the discussions about certain texts that are held in the parlour of Shandy Hall. That Sterne wanted to have his piece chewed over by such a group, fictional or not, is an instance of his urge to step aside from a particular text he has written and speculate on what might happen to it next, and how it might be received. Because *Tristram Shandy* was published in instalments over several years, Sterne was able not only to imagine how later parts of his work might be understood, but could also reflect on how earlier volumes had already been received.

Sterne's first flurry of writing, in the 1741 York by-election, had led to some controversy and embarrassment for Sterne. The result of his second, the *Political Romance*, was brutally suppressed. For some authors, these reactions would have been taken as signs that it was time to give up creative writing altogether. Clearly, the fact that his *Political Romance* had been printed, and stocked in book-shops, albeit briefly, was enough to spur Sterne on to try again.

The Political Club that features in the fuller version of the *Political Romance* recalls the Visitation Dinner in *Tristram Shandy*, at which Walter and Toby try to get a gaggle of drunken, over-fed clerics to answer an abstruse question relating to young Tristram's baptism (*TS* IV, XXVII). A similar discussion-group appears in Sterne's *Rabelaisian Fragment*, which was not published in full until late in the twentieth century. Melvyn New, who edited the *Fragment* for the *Proceedings of the Modern Language Association of America* in 1972, guessed that it dated from that *annus mirabilis* of 1759, when both the *Political Romance* and the first volumes of *Tristram Shandy* appeared.

In the *Fragment*, a group of clerics with Rabelaisian names like Longinus Rabelaicus, Panurge and Triboulet are discussing the idea of publishing a 'Kerukopaedia', a manual of instruction on the art of composing sermons. In the next room, but within earshot, another cleric, called Homenas, is trying to compose a sermon, but is having to resort to stealing ideas from old printed books of sermons by other people. The general discussion in the main room is disturbed by a loud exclamation from Homenas, though the *Fragment* breaks off before the nature of the exclamation is revealed. Sterne re-used this idea in the Visitation Dinner scene of

Tristram Shandy, when Phutatorius, one of the diners, cries 'Zounds' when a hot chestnut falls directly onto his penis.

V. Making Tristram Shandy

In his biography of Sterne, H.D. Traill offers an explanation of why Laurence started to write *Tristram Shandy* in 1759, which may not be entirely accurate, but is certainly entertaining. Sterne, Traill suggests, 'in all likelihood, was in want of money': other motivations included his desire to be famous, and his 'strong and sedulously cultivated taste for Rabelaisian humour'. Sterne's head, Traill guesses, was also 'crammed with all sorts of out-of-the-way learning constantly tickling his comic sense by its very uselessness'.

It is possible that Sterne's Rabelaisian fragment represents some kind of early draft or false start for *Tristram Shandy*. In any case, we know that the author offered an outline for *Tristram* to the London bookseller Robert Dodsley in May 1759. By choosing Dodsley, Sterne was starting at the top: Robert had already published works by Oliver Goldsmith and Samuel Johnson, among others, since he had set up his publishing and book-selling business with the help of Alexander Pope in 1735. For Sterne, Dodsley was also a friend of a friend: Robert's old apprentice John Hinxman now ran a similar operation to Dodsley's at York.

Today, aspiring novelists will find very few publishers willing to accept unsolicited manuscripts for consideration, and very few publishers are also book-sellers, though this was the norm in the eighteenth century, when they were often printers as well. Would-be authors are now advised to contact literary agents with the first fruits of their genius, though very few of those will look at a manuscript sent out of the blue. If the embryonic novelist hears about a likely agent, (s)he will probably need to send an outline and a first chapter: this will be sent on the understanding that the rest of the book is already finished, and in what the author at least considers to be a publishable state.

Since, in the eighteenth century, even quite short books were published a bit at a time, in multiple volumes, publishers seem not to have expected to be given a finished, full-length book in manuscript that they could then chop up into volumes. What Sterne sent Dodsley at the sign of Tully's Head on Pall Mall was a manuscript long enough to fill a first volume of around two hundred and fifty pages, with a letter explaining the project as a whole and a promise to have a second volume ready 'by Christmas, or November', if Dodsley should take the bait. For some reason Sterne asked fifty pounds for the first volume, equivalent to over five thousand pounds today. The closest twenty-first century equivalent to Sterne's approach to Dodsley would perhaps be a script for the pilot of a new TV comedy series, submitted to a production company together with some ideas about how the series might develop over the first few episodes.

Robert Dodsley felt obliged to decline *Tristram Shandy*, especially at such a high price. At the time, he was particularly keen not to be lumbered with a failure, as he was about to retire and pass the business on to his younger brother James. Robert made suggestions as to how Sterne might improve his novel, however, and the author set to work on the important business of revision. Laurence told the reluctant publisher that he was cutting out local references, making the book less of a provincial Yorkshire product. He also lengthened it, making it suitable for publication in two volumes.

The new version of the beginning of *Tristram Shandy* was ready to go to press at the end of 1759, but this time the author did not ask Robert Dodsley to print it. Instead he paid as much as a hundred pounds to have a few hundred copies printed at York, at his own expense. Equivalent to over ten thousand pounds today, Sterne's outlay meant that his decision to self-publish was a considerable gamble. In the twenty-first century, authors with the right technical know-how can self-publish e-books and even hard-copy versions with far less risk, since digital printing means that the cost per copy for short print-runs can be reassuringly low. But even today, self-publishing authors taking the old-fashioned route risk spending a great deal of time and money obtaining a few boxes of copies of their precious book. These, if printed by a sloppy and unscrupulous vanity publisher, have little chance of ever being stocked in a book-shop.

Sterne was very careful to make his self-financed York first edition as saleable as possible. He made sure there was no mention of York on the title page, and modelled the look and quality of the volumes on Robert Dodsley's first edition of Samuel Johnson's novel *Rasselas*, published in April 1759. Sterne took equal care with the subsequent volumes: he was certainly not the kind of author who took no interest in how his work was printed.

Laurence Sterne's own name did not appear anywhere in the volumes, and his real identity was not revealed until some time after publication. As far as the first readers and critics were concerned, the book was written by somebody called Tristram Shandy, or somebody who was using 'Tristram Shandy' as a pen-name.

The York printer Sterne chose to produce the volumes was Ann Ward, who had taken over her business on the death of her husband Caesar in 1759, the year the firm took on *Tristram Shandy*. Sterne knew he could rely on Ann because the Wards had already printed several of his sermons. For over thirty years, Ann also printed the local Tory newspaper, the *York Courant*, as well as sermons by people other than Sterne, reports of trials, guide-books to the local area, and much other material, including works by Francis Drake and John Evelyn. The firm's Coney Street premises were impressive, and even included a room large enough to be used for musical concerts.

Ann Ward was not alone as a woman active in the printing trade in eighteenth-century York. The city's first newspaper, the *York Mercury*, was co-published by one Grace White for two years, until it was taken over by an Alice Bourne. Even the *York Courant* had been printed by a lady called Sarah Coke for a while before the Wards took it over.

The *Shandy*s Ann Ward printed were offered for sale at five shillings by the Dodsleys, and also by another London book-seller, and at the York premises of the aforementioned John Hinxman, the former apprentice of Robert Dodsley. Thanks in part to newspaper adverts, letters and publicity generated by Sterne himself, the first two volumes of *Tristram Shandy* began to sell like hot cakes.

In *The Whitefoord Papers* John Croft tells us that Sterne was quite unaware of the success of the book until he happened to accompany Stephen Croft of Stillington on a trip to London. Croft was clearly looking for company on the trip, and promised to pay all of Sterne's travel expenses. At first the vicar of Stillington refused, saying that he had to stay at home with his wife, but at last he consented, and nipped home to get his best breeches (a truly Shandean detail). Arriving at the Dodsleys' shop in Pall Mall, and asking if they stocked anything written by one Tristram Shandy, Laurence discovered 'that there was not such a Book to be had in London either for Love or money'. *Tristram Shandy* had sold out.

According to Croft, the Dodsleys offered Sterne six hundred pounds for the copyright of the first two volumes of *Tristram*: they planned to bring out a second edition as soon as possible. Croft's figure is certainly an exaggeration: the Dodsleys paid two hundred and fifty pounds for the right to print a new edition of the first two volumes in London. By using more than one printer, the Dodsleys managed to get five thousand copies ready by the second of April 1760. The new edition had a dedication to the then Prime Minister, William Pitt, expressing the hope that this 'great sir' would be able to take *Tristram Shandy* into the country with him 'where, if I am ever told, it has made you smile; or can conceive it has beguiled you of one moment's pain – I shall think myself as happy as a minister of state'.

The new edition also had an engraving after an original by William Hogarth, opposite the front page. To get Hogarth on board was certainly a coup for Sterne and the Dodsleys, and an indication of how famous *Tristram* already was, on the basis of the few hundred copies that were the maximum that could have been sold up to this point. Hogarth's engraving shows the episode from volume two where Corporal Trim, his body inclined at a very particular angle, reads Yorick's sermon to uncle Toby, Tristram's father, and Dr Slop. In the picture, the man-midwife, who is so short that his feet do not touch the ground, is asleep in his chair. The brothers Shandy are smoking, and there is a map of the fortifications of Namur hanging on the wall in the background.

Hogarth himself is mentioned in chapter nine of Sterne's second volume, where the artist's book *The Analysis of Beauty*, published in 1753, is mentioned. Sterne suggests that if the reader has not yet read Hogarth's book, he certainly should. Elsewhere in *Tristram*, Sterne mentions the Line of Beauty, an idea of Hogarth's that Sterne must have got from his own reading of the artist's book. Since various squiggly lines appear as illustrations in *Tristram Shandy*, it is tempting to suggest that Sterne included them partly to satirise Hogarth's idea. None of Sterne's lines conform to the gentle 'S' shape of Hogarth's perfect Line of Beauty, which is shown in the well-known self-portrait of the artist with his pet dog. If he had any choice in the matter, Hogarth may have chosen Trim's reading of the sermon as a subject because Sterne tells us in chapter seventeen of his second volume that as he read the sermon Trim's 'knee bent, but that not violently, but so as to fall within the limits of the line of beauty'.

The new London edition of *Tristram* made it possible for far more people to read the start of Sterne's novel, but since it was priced at four shillings, by no means everyone could own a copy. Four shillings in 1760 was the equivalent of over twenty pounds today: the printers in the Dodsleys' employ would have been lucky to earn that sum in two days. Cash-strapped readers may also have been put off paying such a sum for what was only part of a book: how much would they have to invest to possess the whole thing? How many volumes would *Tristram Shandy* stretch to?

Some people who could have afforded to buy the first two volumes of *Tristram Shandy* may not have been sufficiently literate to understand it – it was never intended to be an easy read, and the significance of some of Sterne's allusions still puzzle scholars. Perhaps half of King George II's subjects were completely illiterate, and could only have learned about Sterne's novel by reputation.

It is puzzling to imagine how an enthusiastic early reader of *Tristram Shandy* would describe it to, for instance, a semi-literate maid. Even an anonymous reviewer writing in the *Critical Review* in January 1760 found the book hard to describe, even though an important part of his or her job consisted in describing books, and even though he or she was writing for a readership who were already sufficiently well-informed about literature to want to read reviews of new books.

The Critical Reviewer wrote, 'This is a humorous performance, of which we are unable to convey any distinct ideas to our readers'. The review then contradicts itself by offering a very creditable account of the overall structure of the first two volumes: 'The whole is composed of digressions, divertingly enough introduced, and characters which we think well supported'. The reviewer then resorts to picking out some of the humorous characters and incidents, much as a modern person might do, while describing the book to a friend:

Nothing can be more ridiculous than uncle *Toby*'s embarrassment in describing the siege of Namur, *Trim*'s attitude reading aloud a sermon, and Dr. *Slop*'s overthrow in the rencounter with Obadiah the coachman.

As we shall see, this same anonymous reviewer pointed out the similarities between *Tristram Shandy* and *Peregrine Pickle*, a novel first published by Tobias Smollett in 1751. Here *Peregrine* is not named, however, but merely alluded to as 'a modern truly Cervantic performance'. Smollett himself must have known about this notice, since he edited the *Critical Review*.

Other reviewers had less trouble giving an account of *Tristram Shandy*. William Kenrick, writing in the *Monthly Review*, mentioned 'a certain quaintness, and something like an affectation of being immoderately witty, throughout the whole work' which he found 'entertaining'. Kenrick wound up his review by saying that the author of *Tristram Shandy* was 'a writer infinitely more ingenious and entertaining than any other of the present race of novelists'.

Some disagreed, believing the book to be indelicate, but even Horace Walpole, who found *Tristram Shandy* 'insipid and tedious' had to admit that 'at present nothing is talked of, nothing admired' except Sterne's volumes. Sterne himself wrote, 'one half of the town abuse my book as bitterly, as the other half cry it up to the skies – the best is, they abuse it and buy it'. It was said that the book was so talked about that, because *Tristram Shandy* associated sex with the winding up of a clock, the London prostitutes took to offering to wind up the clocks of prospective clients.

VI. Coxwold, York, London, France and Italy

Whatever else he expected from writing such a book, it is unlikely that Laurence Sterne thought that *Tristram Shandy* would bring him preferment in the Church. But that it did, in the form of another living, this time at Coxwold, a Yorkshire village like Sutton and Stillington, some ten miles north and a little west of the latter, and around eighteen miles north of York itself . The living had become free on the death of the aforementioned Richard Wilkinson, the previous incumbent, who had once worked as Sterne's curate at Sutton-in-the-Forest. The new living, which may have brought Sterne another seventy pounds a year, was presented to him by the local lord of the manor, Thomas Belasyse, Earl Fauconberg. The Earl owned Newburgh Priory, a fine house near Coxwold which, like Sterne's parsonage, can still be visited (technically Sterne's new home was not a parsonage, as it was rented by incumbents from the noble Earl).

Thomas Belasyse, who evidently relished the idea of having the author of *Tristram Shandy* as a near neighbour in the country, was not the only one who wanted to know and befriend the newly-famous Sterne. During those glittering weeks of the first flush of Sterne's fame in London, he became friends with the celebrated actor David Garrick, some ladies of the royal bedchamber, and various lords, bishops and other luminaries. Lord Rockingham presented him at Court, where he met the Duke of York. For a writer, the most flattering of these new friendships must surely have been the one he struck up with the elderly Lord Allen Bathurst, who had known Alexander Pope, Jonathan Swift, Joseph Addison and Richard Steele. Although Bathurst would have been well into his seventies when he introduced himself to Sterne at the Princess of Wales's Court, Allen still managed to outlive Laurence, dying in 1775 at the age of ninety.

Another older associate who also managed to live longer than Sterne was William Warburton, a bishop of Gloucester whom Edward Gibbon described as 'the Dictator and Tyrant of the World of Literature'. At first, Warburton praised *Tristram Shandy*, recommended it to his fellow bishops, among others, and even presented its author with a purse of gold, an outré gesture that seems to belong more in a Shakespeare play than in the biography of an eighteenth-century parson. But when there was talk of Warburton being satirised in later volumes of *Tristram*, the bishop's enthusiasm cooled. Concerned that the projected future volumes might be too bawdy, he advised Sterne to avoid 'violations of decency and good manners', and eventually began to refer to the author in his letters as 'an irrecoverable scoundrel' and 'that egregious Puppy'.

Thanks to Fauconberg's gift of the living of Coxwold, it was to that Yorkshire village that Sterne returned in May 1760, when he felt he could not decently extend his stay in London any further. The place was certainly better for his health than London, but by December he was bored with it. He could, however, write there, and of course there were further volumes of *Tristram Shandy* to complete. Laurence had the time to do this because many of his priestly duties in Yorkshire were now farmed out to sometimes poorly-qualified curates and other substitutes.

The burden that fell on those who earned a meagre living standing in for Sterne was increased when the author's tuberculosis began to give him serious trouble in the autumn of 1761. Although his income from sales of *Tristram*, of which book there were now four volumes, and from his published sermons, was seldom impressive enough to allow Sterne to regard himself as a rich man, the author was now prosperous enough to contemplate travelling south for the sake of his health. He was also able to plan a similar migration for his wife and daughter: Lydia, who was now a young teenager, probably suffered from asthma.

Sterne set out for France in the first week of January 1762, although technically England was at war with that country. Despite his medical need to spend the winter further south, he stayed in Paris for some six months. There he was delighted to be fêted and lionised much as he had been in London in 1760. Few of his new French friends could have read Sterne's *Tristram Shandy*: no French translation was published until after the author's death; but the literati of Paris had heard of the book, which had become famous, if not notorious, in many parts of Europe. As in London, various aristocrats invited the Englishman to the meetings of their coteries. Sterne also attended the theatre, concerts and the opera, visited Versailles and wrote enthusiastic letters home, particularly to David Garrick.

Perhaps the best-known new friend Sterne made in Paris was the writer and philosopher Denis Diderot, who was born in 1713, the same year as Sterne, and would have been around fifty when they first met. Diderot's name is forever coupled with that of his colleague Jean le Rond d'Alembert, with whom he collaborated on the French *Encyclopédie*, the great enlightenment project. In France, various attempts were made to suppress the *Encyclopédie,* which was regarded by many as dangerously anti-Christian. This means that when Sterne and Diderot met, they were both writers whose controversial works had not yet been published in their entirety: the *Encyclopédie* was not completed until after Sterne's death. Later, Diderot would write controversial novels, including *The Nun* and *Jacques the Fatalist*, the latter influenced by Sterne.

The *Encyclopédie* is referred to in chapter nine of the second volume of *Tristram Shandy*, where Sterne suggests that Corporal Trim's posture when reading out a sermon in the parlour of Shandy Hall:

shall be commented upon in that part of the cyclopædia of arts and sciences, where the instrumental parts of the eloquence of the senate, the pulpit, and the bar, the coffee-house, the bed-chamber, and fire-side, fall under consideration.

The implication here is that the 'cyclopædia' will be so detailed that it will include everything, right down to the details of completely trivial events that once took place in obscure country houses in England. This is a truly Swiftian notion: in his *Gulliver's Travels*, Jonathan Swift toyed with ideas such as gigantic maps made to the same scale as the lands they represented.

Sterne may also have been satirising Diderot and d'Alembert's *Encyclopédie* with his *Tristra-pædia*; a book supposed to contain everything Walter Shandy feels that his second son should learn, but which Walter himself cannot write quickly enough for it to be of any use. In *Tristram Shandy*, Tristram, the supposed author, also complains that he will never finish writing the story of his life because he is actually living his life while he writes it, and will never be able to catch up with himself.

Sterne made Diderot a generous gift of English books while he was in Paris, including the whole of *Tristram Shandy* up to that point, and the complete works of the poet Alexander Pope.

Sterne's wife and daughter arrived in Paris in July 1762, and the small family had soon departed for the supposedly healthier climate of the south. From this time until nearly the end of May 1764, when Sterne returned to England alone, the Sternes tried various places in France, including Montpellier, Toulouse, Marseilles and Aix-en-Provence. They were concerned to find somewhere that was healthy for all of them, where they could live cheaply, and where there was a reasonable number of English visitors of the right class, for company. Sterne's poor French made it difficult for him to sustain a sophisticated conversation in that language.

On his travels, Sterne was still able to add to *Tristram Shandy*, though news of sales from England was not always encouraging. Some of the critics who wrote about the later volumes still insisted that they were too bawdy, especially to have come from the pen of a clergyman, and some even said that the book was flagging, and becoming dull.

During his travels, and indeed for the rest of his life, Sterne endured periods where his tuberculosis was very bad: he often suffered from episodes when the blood-vessels in his lungs bled copiously; something that the doctors of the time attempted to treat by drawing off more blood from the patient's arms. After less than eighteen months alone in England (he had left Elizabeth and Lydia in France) he headed south again, this time determined to cross the Alps and reach Italy.

Italy agreed with Sterne: there, he enjoyed good health and even noticed that he was gaining weight. The Italians can have understood even less than the French about the real nature of Sterne's achievement as a writer, but he was still fêted as a celebrated author.

At Florence, his portrait was painted by the English artist Thomas Patch, who produced a macabre caricature of the author as *Tristram Shandy*, confronting Death in the form of a skeleton complete with scythe and winged hour-glass. Patch was inspired by an episode at the start of volume seven of *Tristram*, where Death interrupts the hero as he is talking to his friend Eugenius (code name for Sterne's real friend John Hall-Stevenson). After calling Death 'this *son of a whore*' Tristram decides to run away from him 'to the banks of the *Garonne*', then to mount Vesuvius, Joppa and 'the world's end'.

Sterne did indeed see Mount Vesuvius during his Italian travels: in fact he was lucky enough to see it while it was active. He stayed for a while at nearby Naples, and also visited Rome, where the English sculptor Joseph Nollekens made a marble bust of the author. After a brief visit to his wife and daughter at Fontette near Dijon in France, Sterne was back in England in June 1766. Volume nine, the last section of *Tristram Shandy*, was finished at Coxwold and published in London in January 1767.

VII. Tristram Shandy I: Overview

What is there left to be said about a book about which so much has been written already? Perhaps it is best to stick to the obvious.

Tristram Shandy is written as the autobiography of a fictitious character, the fictitious narrator being Tristram himself. It is delightful to think that every year a certain number of people must pick up the book thinking that it will be exactly what its title says it is: the life and opinions of Tristram Shandy, gentleman. Such unsuspecting readers probably expect a first chapter on the narrator's forbears, followed by a chapter on his birth and early childhood, with later chapters on his school-days, his time at college, first love, and first steps on a career.

If such unsuspecting readers understand that the book is a novel, they probably expect some element of conflict or difficulty – in short, the beginnings of a story – to begin to appear early on. The perfect example of this kind of thing can be found in Charles Dickens' novel *Great Expectations*, first published in book form in 1861. The second paragraph of the book comprises the narrator's brief account of the only forbears he has any knowledge of: his parents and all but one of his siblings. Since they all lie buried in the local churchyard, the second paragraph of *Great Expectations* includes a description of their grave-stones, and the whimsical impressions the narrator has of them.

After the first three paragraphs of Dickens' book, Pip, the orphaned hero, encounters the terrifying Abel Magwitch, an escaped convict. Although he doesn't realise this for many years, his secret childhood involvement with Magwitch radically changes the whole course of Pip's life. Instead of growing up into the blacksmith's trade (the profession of his amiable brother-in-law) Pip has 'great expectations', and a private income, and is to learn to be a gentleman.

Although Sterne's *Tristram Shandy* does give some account of Tristram's forbears, these hints are scattered in various corners of the novel, and the book actually opens with the narrator's *conception*. This is unconventional to say the least, and must have been disconcerting to some strait-laced early readers of Sterne. What *is* conventional about this bold opening is that it immediately introduces the necessary element of conflict into the novel. Tristram tells us that because *something went wrong* during his conception, his own mind and body have never been quite right. If his conception had gone better, 'I am verily persuaded I should have made a quite different figure in the world from that in which the reader is likely to see me'.

What went wrong with the conception is that, presumably at the moment of ejaculation, Tristram's mother interrupted her husband with the distracting question, 'Pray, my Dear, have you not forgot to wind up the clock?' This, according to the narrator, compromised the transfusion of the 'animal spirits' from father to son; which is most unfortunate, because 'nine parts in ten of a man's sense or his nonsense, his successes and miscarriages in this world depend upon their [meaning the animal spirits'] motions and activity'.

Readers are therefore warned on the very first page that Tristram Shandy's story is going to be the story of a man oddly cursed (though in a comical way) not just from birth, but from his very conception. Later we learn that little Tristram has also inherited the hereditary bad luck of the Shandy family; which might, of course, have caused his mother to ask her disastrous question in the first place.

When writers use the first person to tell the story of another person, whether fictional or real-life, they are obliged to perform like actors, though they use their writing skills to do this, and not make-up, costumes, gestures and facial expressions. *What* the fictional 'I' says is important, but *how he says it* can also reveal extra layers of meaning. Writing *Tristram Shandy*, Laurence Sterne not only wrote *as* a man cursed with 'a thousand weaknesses both of body and mind': he wrote his book in the style that such a man might have employed.

This idea of writing a book in a style that suits the content seems not to have been understood by Sterne's critic and contemporary Horace Walpole, who wrote the influential *Castle of Otranto* (1764). Said to be the first gothic novel, *Otranto* comprises a twisted tale of ghostly revenge, bizarre visions, dark dungeons, mysterious deaths, and the incestuous longings of old men for helpless young virgins. Despite its sensational content, the style of Walpole's shocker is inappropriately measured, balanced and sedate. Reading it, one feels one is watching a sensational melodrama performed by actors who are half-asleep.

The idea of opening with a sense of the hero's misfortunes, as used in *Tristram Shandy*, is hardly new. In the first lines of John Dryden's version of Virgil's *Aeneid*, we learn that the hero, Aeneas, is not going to have an easy time of it:

Arms, and the man I sing, who, forc'd by fate,
And haughty Juno's unrelenting hate,
Expell'd and exil'd, left the Trojan shore.
Long labours, both by sea and land, he bore . . .

In the first pages of *Tristram Shandy*, readers are acquainted with the fact that Tristram is not only cursed: he is also going to confide in us about all sorts of things, including some embarrassing personal matters relating to himself and his family. The narrator is also very forthcoming about how he intends to write his book, how and when he writes, the difficulties he encounters while writing, what he wears when writing, and even how the reader should read the resulting book. He never conceals the fact that his is going to be a very odd book. At the end of chapter six we are given fair warning:

As you proceed farther with me, the slight acquaintance, which is now beginning betwixt us . . . will terminate in friendship . . . then nothing which has touched me will be thought trifling in its nature, or tedious in its telling. Therefore, my dear friend and companion, if you should think me somewhat sparing of my narrative on my first setting out - bear with me, - and let me go on, and tell my story my own way: - Or, if I should seem now and then to trifle upon the road, or should sometimes put on a fool's cap with a bell to it, for a moment or two as we pass along, - don't fly off, - but rather courteously give me credit for a little more wisdom than appears upon my outside . . .

The warning does not appear very far into the book – Sterne's chapters are often very short.

Tristram is 'sparing of [his] narrative' because it proceeds slowly, interspersed with many digressions and reflections, as the early critics noticed. The reader is politely asked to 'bear with' these diversions, because of the friendship he will form with the author. As the author's friend, the reader will value his eccentric approach to writing, because to a friend of Tristram's 'nothing which has touched me will be thought trifling in its nature, or tedious in its telling'.

Elsewhere, Tristram is not so confident that his approach reflects 'more wisdom than appears upon my outside'. After a digression about a lame man who repeatedly stands up when he should sit down (to rest his bad leg), the author declares 'But this is neither here nor there - why do I mention it? - Ask my pen, - it governs me, - I govern not it' (*TS* VI, VI).

Much later in the novel Tristram describes how a more conventional form of story-telling can be depicted as a straight horizontal line on the page. To describe his own technique, he requires a series of squiggly diagrams to be reproduced, representing the pattern of each of the five books he has written so far. The last of these has letters marking particular diversions from the straight line: the letters correspond to short descriptions of the diversions in the narrative that they represent (*TS* VI, XL).

One reason for the slow progress of the central narrative is the author's aforementioned tendency to digress. Many of the digressions that veer off from the narrative of Tristram's birth are explanatory as well as humorous. We learn that, unusually, Tristram's mother was attended by two midwives while she was giving birth to the fictitious narrator. The reasons for this are explained at length, as is the reason how and why one of the midwives became a midwife in the first place. Otherwise, we learn little of this midwife, an unnamed middle-aged widow who lives locally: we learn far more about Doctor Slop, the second midwife, a bow-legged Roman Catholic dwarf who fancies himself a scientist, having written and published on the subject of midwifery.

It is a commonplace that in England, until fairly recently, men were not present in the room when their children were born. Old-fashioned films and TV dramas would often show the expectant father pacing about in some other room in the home or hospital, looking worried, smoking copious cigarettes and listening out for the tell-tale yowl of the new-born. In *Tristram Shandy*, the business of the men waiting for the birth is described at great length.

While Mrs Shandy is giving birth upstairs, most of the action downstairs is centred on the parlour. There Walter, Tristram's father, sits with his younger brother Toby, who is perhaps the most attractive character in the entire canon of English literature. Toby's servant Corporal Trim is often in attendance, and because he is only to help out with the birth if there is an emergency and he is called for, Doctor Slop spends many pages in the room as well.

The conversation in the room is very eccentric and wide-ranging. The mood of the master of the house, Walter Shandy, is grim not because he fears that something will go wrong with the birth, but because he is convinced that, because his conception was interrupted, his child will be cursed; an opinion which, as we have seen, is later shared by his unfortunate son. Walter's brother Toby offers the comfort of good, plain sense, but his entire sense of what is happening in the room, the house and the world in general is coloured by what Tristram calls his 'hobby-horse'; his obsession with all things military.

The amount of time various characters are able to spend talking, listening and even sleeping in the parlour of Shandy Hall during Tristram's birth is a reminder that this book is set in the eighteenth century and not the twenty-first. The idea of a modern midwife, whether male or female, keeping company for hours with the father of the child being born, while there is another midwife in attendance, seems odd from our modern perspective. The idea that the discovery of a forgotten sermon would lead to its being read aloud in its entirety straight away also seems bizarre: today few of us have the leisure – or the empty hours to fill – of the old country gentry, with their servants and their eccentric hobbies.

Yorick, the local parson, is a frequent guest at Shandy Hall: his visits seem not to have any particular purpose – he just 'hangs out' with the Shandy family, perhaps because they are among the few people in the neighbourhood who count as 'polite society'. His modern equivalent, the Anglican vicar trying desperately to stretch himself over several widely-scattered parishes, would hardly have time for such frequent, leisurely visits to the house of just one family of parishioners, if he or she took his or her job seriously.

Although the Shandys are not as grand as Sir Roger de Coverley, Yorick's role as a clerical 'extra', companion or unofficial chaplain at Shandy Hall reminds one of Sir Roger's specifications for a local cleric. A comic creation of the writer Joseph Addison who first appeared in *The Spectator* in 1711, Sir Roger requires a clergyman who will not embarrass him by using Greek or Latin at the dinner-table; 'a clergyman rather of plain sense than much learning, of a good aspect, a clear voice, a sociable temper, and, if possible, a man that understood a little of backgammon'.

Addison's Sir Roger is keen to preserve his own peace of mind, at least in the choice of a chaplain, and there is a sense in *Tristram Shandy* that the parlour at Shandy Hall, for all its bizarre goings-on, is at least potentially a haven of peace and brotherly love. It is generally peaceful enough for people (meaning men) to make a habit of dozing off there, and it is certainly cut off, to some extent, from the tumultuous life of the room upstairs, where Elizabeth Shandy is giving birth.

It is to Shandy Hall that Walter has escaped from business life in London, and here Toby has found refuge from his hard and dangerous life in the army. The threats that might be more evident far from this house, this parlour, and England itself, are brought home to us by Sterne's reminders of the fate of Corporal Trim's brother Tom, a prisoner of the Inquisition in Portugal. Even the dangers of the troubled seventeenth century in England are brought to mind by Tristram's mention of his great-uncle 'Mr. *Hammond Shandy*, - a little man, - but of high fancy: - he rushed into the duke of *Monmouth's* affair' (*TS* III, X). In the past, and perhaps the future, and in other places, trouble can be found; but here and now in the parlour of Shandy Hall there is at least some shelter.

Whether it is hard-earned or not, the relative idleness of Walter Shandy and Parson Yorick may seem indefensible in our busy age. Are they 'status dropouts', a class of men described by the American writer Tom Wolfe in an essay printed in his 1968 book *The Pump House Gang*? The king of the status dropouts, according to Wolfe, was the rich proprietor of a highly profitable pornographic magazine, who, having made his fortune, did little work to maintain it, seldom bothered to show his face at 'society' events, and merely fooled around and had fun. It may be that Walter and Yorick are such men, but their apparent pointlessness has also to be viewed through the lens of the gentlemanly ideal of the English in those days. To become a real gentleman, not obliged to work, was seen as an admirable accomplishment, to be attained at all costs.

Tristram, the supposed author of the book, seems to have inherited this leisurely lifestyle along with his father's house and fortune. He has certainly found time to do a number of things modern people might only do if they had unusual quantities of time on their hands. As well as amusing himself by writing *Tristram Shandy* itself, he reads all of Yorick's sermons, the texts of which are kept at Shandy Hall. He also reads widely in his father's library, which, he tells us, 'was not great, but to make amends, it was curious' (*TS* III, XXV). There is also a hint that he plans to publish his father's own writings. The reader doubts, however, that Tristram will ever get around to arranging for the creaking hinge of the parlour door to be oiled.

Thanks to Tristram's accounts of the conversations in the parlour, which, as we have seen, are also broken up by characters reading aloud from written texts, stories-within-the-story and explanatory digressions, this long novel of nearly two hundred thousand words is half over before the hero has even been christened. Time, as it unfolds around the hero, is not treated with any consistency. At one point, the narrative jumps forward several years to the occasion when the hero is accidentally circumcised by a falling sash-window. The comical reason why the sash fell is explained in detail, and the comic potential of a circumcised boy in a house full of Gentiles is subtly exploited. The comedy then leaps ahead again, to Tristram's attempt to improve his health, as Sterne did, by travelling on the Continent. We then return to Shandy Hall and its environs for what Tristram has long promised us will be the best part of his book: the courtship of his uncle Toby and a neighbouring widow, Mrs Wadman.

Sterne's use of digressions in *Tristram Shandy* makes it possible for him to bring a great deal of comical, bizarre and sometimes obscene matter into his book. Some of the digressions, subtly edited, might do perfectly well as stand-alone tales in, say, an anthology of comical eighteenth-century prose. As Tristram implies in his advice to the reader, quoted above, the reader must be open-minded and accept his digressions on their own terms. He must not 'fly off' or skip pages just to get back to the 'main narrative'. The digressions are the whole point: the term 'main narrative' is only used here as a convenient stop-gap. The book is remarkably democratic in that everything and everybody in it is shown to be equally important, and also equally unimportant and comically futile.

Because of its unusual structure – the odd way in which it manipulates both time and space – some readers cannot cope with *Tristram Shandy* at all. Students of English Literature tend to come across it for the first time during degree-level courses, and one suspects that many an undergraduate essay on the novel has been written by students who have only read about it, and have not actually read it. On a sentence-by-sentence basis Sterne's prose in *Tristram Shandy* is usually no more difficult than that of many other eighteenth-century writers, but the unexpected form the book takes frustrates some readers who have a perhaps unconscious but nonetheless rigid sense of what a novel should be.

It is a mistake to assume that because it seems ramshackle, and is indeed unpredictable, *Tristram Shandy* lacks structure. In recent years, critics such as Freeman (2002) have spotted a *fractal* structure in the book. Fractals are complex pictorial representations of mathematical formulae, usually generated using computer software. One of the most famous, the Mandelbrot Set, is a three-dimensional picture, infinite in all dimensions, where a single shape endlessly repeats itself, for instance by 'budding off' from itself. Although 'our cold maids' might think that the basic Mandelbrot shape looks like a cross-section of an apple, Sterne and Shakespeare's 'liberal shepherds' would surely see the similarity to a pair of buttocks.

Fractal patterns appear in nature as well as on computers and in mathematics: the typical tree, for instance, repeats the pattern of 'branch splits into two or more branches' until the branches become twigs. Whereas in the Mandelbrot Set the basic shape looks like a an apple or a backside, in *Tristram Shandy* the building-block is an amusing story that is either cut short or fizzles out, leaving the reader delightfully mystified, or frustrated. Something like the novel's fractal structure was described by no less a figure than Edmund Burke, in a review published in the *Annual Register* for 1760. The novel's digressions, he wrote, 'so frequently repeated, instead of relieving the reader, become at length tiresome. The book is a perpetual series of disappointments'.

In his essay in the journal *Studies in the Novel*, John Freeman notes how Sterne's own diagrams of his chapters resemble fractals, and how uncle Toby's scale models of siege fortifications themselves look like snow-flakes, which in turn resemble fractals.

VIII. Tristram Shandy II: Setting

Despite its bizarre and, to some, frustrating structure, *Tristram Shandy* still shares elements with more conventional novels, such as settings, characters and plot. Of the three, perhaps the most conventional element in Sterne's novel is the setting.

Most of the novel takes place in and around Shandy Hall, the home of Tristram's father Walter and his wife, Tristram's mother. Whereas other authors might have lingered for at least a page over a systematic and evocative description of the place, Sterne opts not to do so. He does not even allow the reader to overhear a conversation about the general state of the house and the land around it. This shows the extent to which the author relies on characters to tell his story, and trusts that readers will draw on their own imaginations to supply the background to his comic scenes. The lack of description of Shandy Hall may also be a function of the dramatic character of the book. Here, we read scenes played out against a backdrop, as in a theatre. Nobody comes onto the stage during a play and describes the set.

This is quite different to the approach of Sterne's friend John Hall Stevenson, who begins his *Crazy Tales* with a description of his castle, then in disrepair:

> A turret also you may note,
> Its glory vanished like a dream,
> Transformed into a pigeon-cote,

Nodding beside the sleepy stream.

From what we can gather about Shandy Hall it is a real, lived-in house of the period. It is possible to visit English eighteenth-century country houses today, but organisations such as the National Trust have sometimes been criticised for turning such houses, or at least parts of them, into sparkling show-houses that lack that genuine lived-in feel. Such houses may now be centrally-heated: all the old fireplaces have been sealed, and are home to sprays of flowers or decorative fans. Because they are supposed to be eighteenth-century houses, there are no longer any pictures or pieces of furniture in them that do not come from that century. No visitors will see the fine seventeenth-century oak staircase, now used as a fire-escape, unless there is an actual fire, and the once-celebrated Victorian billiard-room is now behind a door marked 'PRIVATE' and is used as the staff canteen.

The perceived necessity of presenting a 'consistent' 'period' house for coach-loads of visitors, and the occasional film-crew, sometimes makes those in charge of eighteenth-century English country houses forget that many of the real gentry of the eighteenth century would have thought it outrageous to buy, or have made, a new bed when the old, Tudor one was still perfectly serviceable. By the same token, they would not have taken the stiff, formal fifteenth-century portrait of an ancestor out of their first-floor gallery simply because it looked old. They were far more likely to repair or refurbish such objects than to replace them.

Period showhouses, masquerading as genuine country houses from Sterne's time, will often have immaculate gardens, tended by armies of enthusiastic local volunteers. Beyond the gardens are fields used as car-parks for summer visitors, and other fields housing picturesque animals, such as deer or alpacas. By contrast, Sterne's Shandy Hall has other people's gardens, and a relative's notable re-purposed bowling-green, within easy reach of the front door. There is also the matter of the Ox-moor, described as 'a fine, large, whinny, undrained, unimproved common, belonging to the *Shandy*-estate', which Tristrams's father 'had long and

54

affectionately set his heart upon turning . . . to some account' (*TS* IV, XXXI).

Another example of unfinished business around the old place is the aforementioned creaking hinge on the door to the parlour. Somebody should have oiled this years ago (with a feather acting as a brush to apply the oil, suggests Tristram), and it might even have been worthwhile to call in a blacksmith to actually repair it, but it is still creaking horribly when Tristram sits down in that very parlour to write his *Life and Opinions*. For years, Tristram explains, it interfered with his father's after-dinner naps, and the creak is so loud that, to avoid it, servants and others have established a tradition of leaving the door ajar. This open door policy has a benign side-effect, in that anyone happening to pause outside can listen to the conversation inside. This is a great convenience for the servants, and for Tristram's mother. Tristram promises, however, that it will be fixed during the reign of the monarch sitting on the throne while he is writing his book.

The Shandy family's delays over sorting out the Ox-moor and the hinge are very realistic touches. People who own their homes will generally have various improvement projects on hold, which might never actually be completed. In a modern house or flat, these might include double-glazing the whole place (as Sterne 'sashed' his first parsonage), replacing a cracked sink, and installing cupboards for the clothes which have been sitting in cardboard boxes since the occupants moved in.

Tristram is quite clear that the delay over improving the Ox-moor is partly due to a lack of funds. It seems that Tristram's father cannot even consider reclaiming the moor until he inherits a thousand pounds from his aunt Dinah. Then he is thrown into an agony of indecision: should he indeed invest the money in the moor, or should he use it to fund his older son Bobby's Grand Tour? It is clear that he cannot consider doing both. This is a shame, since eighteenth-century landlords were increasing their incomes at this time by reclaiming such land and cultivating it using the latest scientific methods. Tristram tells us that his father calculated that:

it was plain he should reap a hundred lasts of rape, at twenty pounds a last, the very first year - besides an excellent crop of wheat the year following - and the year after that, to speak within bounds, a hundred - but in all likelihood, a hundred and fifty - if not two hundred quarters of pease and beans - besides potatoes without end. -

The detail Sterne is able to go into in the passage above probably reflects his own experience as an (unsuccessful) small-scale farmer, and may also include information remembered from conversations with neighbouring land-owners and tenant farmers. Sterne was also involved in various enclosure schemes: in the eighteenth century, these involved the legalised theft of common land from local peasants, who had enjoyed ancient rights to its use. Once land-owners had appropriated such lands, they were free to improve them using the latest methods.

There is further evidence of the comparative poverty of the Shandy family in the fact that there seem to be very few servants, and each of these are expected to turn their hands to different tasks – in a larger establishment, there would be more specialisation. At one point, we see Walter Shandy being dressed by Susannah, one of the maids (*TS* IV, XIV): in a really grand house, this would of course have been done by a male valet. As if to mislead the reader, Sterne throws us into the middle of this scene, so that Walter's command to Susannah, to reach him his breeches, makes us think that the two of them have just been having sex. This may reflect some memory of Sterne's dalliances with, or abuse of, his own household maids. The scene also suggests some of the inconveniences of using a maid-of-all-work as a valet: she is likely to be called away for other duties; in this case assisting at the complicated birth of Tristram himself.

As well as the multi-tasking servants at Shandy Hall, there is a lack of specialisation in the matter of the family horses. When a servant called Obadiah is called upon to ride as quickly as possible to Dr Slop's house, he is obliged to ride 'a strong monster of a coach-horse' (*TS* II, IX).

The fact that a house very near Shandy Hall, and certainly situated in its grounds, is rented to a genteel widow is further evidence of the comparative poverty of the Shandys. The tenant is the beautiful Widow Wadman, who sets her cap at uncle Toby. She may be living in an old dower house of the estate, or perhaps a hunting-lodge, a gate-house or even converted stables. In any case, a really wealthy county family would not have had to rent out such a place.

It is instructive to compare the way of life at Shandy Hall to that of the aforementioned Sir Roger de Coverley, Addison's fictional creation who appeared in early numbers of *The Spectator*. Sir Roger's country house has a fine gallery full of portraits of his forebears, going back several generations. He keeps at least one superb pack of hunting-dogs, and is so keen on fox-hunting that he has 'extra' foxes, captured in surrounding counties, released onto his land. He regularly hands out 'bounties', meaning gifts of various kinds, to his tenants, and, as we have seen, he can afford to keep his own chaplain. He buys a complete set of all the worthwhile sermons ever written in English and makes a gift of them to the local parson, and when he visits London he is able to live in style, visit all the best coffee-houses and attend the theatre. To judge from his surname, Sir Roger comes from an old Norman family. He is a local Justice of the Peace and has been Member of Parliament for his constituency several times. By contrast, the only service Walter Shandy offers to the neighbourhood is the loan of his bull 'for the service of the Parish'. Tristram is not sure whether his father does this 'by ancient custom of the manor, or as impropriator of the great tithes' (*TS* IX, XXXIII).

Looking after a bull at his own expense was a traditional role for a local land-owner. Bulls are large, aggressive and both dangerous and expensive to keep. Apart from their indispensable role in impregnating cows, they are also pretty useless, until they die or are slaughtered, and can be eaten, and their hides used for leather. By lending out this expensive item to local farmers, the local landowner would acquire prestige, earn gratitude and make lesser farmers feel obliged to him.

One problem with this arrangement (apart from the expense and danger of keeping the bull itself) is that the whole business has a slightly bawdy, Rabelaisian side. Like so much else connected with the Shandys, their willingness to loan out their bull is distinctly embarrassing; one certainly would not talk about it, in too much detail, in the company of small children. The parish bull, which is only mentioned right at the end of the book, is also comically disappointing and futile. 'The parish being very large,' Tristram tells us, 'my father's Bull, to speak the truth of him, was no way equal to the department'. This revelation is vouchsafed shortly after there has been a great deal of 'bustle' in the novel over whether Tristram's uncle Toby might have been rendered impotent by his injury sustained at the Siege of Namur in 1692. Sterne deliberately mixes up uncle Toby's injury with the possible impotence or sterility of the parish bull, and the pregnancy of one of the Shandy Hall servants.

As we have seen, although he is a keen reader and fancies himself as a scholar, Walter Shandy has to content himself with a small but 'curious' library of volumes that deal directly with subjects with which he is perhaps unhealthily obsessed. Not for him one of the vast libraries of gold-tooled calf-bound volumes visitors ogle in the best country houses. While Sir Roger de Coverley's income flows effortlessly from his extensive lands, Tristram's father has been forced to restore, or perhaps found, the Shandy family fortunes by speculating in foreign trade.

It is unclear whether Shandy Hall, the setting for so much of Sterne's novel, has been in the family for several generations, was bought by Tristram's father when he had become sufficiently wealthy in 'the Turkey trade', whether Walter inherited it, or whether it stood empty, or was rented by strangers, until the Shandys could afford to live in it again. In any case, it is interesting that uncle Toby, as a wounded army captain, is able to leave London and occupy his own house near Shandy Hall before his older brother becomes rich enough to retire from business and live permanently in the Hall itself.

At the time of their marriage, we are told, Tristram's mother insists on a clause in the marriage contract that gives her the right to spend her pregnant months in London, if she happens to fall pregnant when her husband has left off business:

in order to retire to, and dwell upon, his estate at *Shandy Hall*, in the county of -----, or at any other country-seat, castle, hall, mansion-house, messuage or grainge-house . . .

(*TS* I, XV)

This suggests that, during their courtship in London, his bride already suspected Walter of yearning to bury himself down in the country.

The fact that the Shandys do not have very deep pockets, do not tower over their genteel neighbours, are probably not in possession of that magical thing, 'old money', and perhaps live in a modest, even ramshackle excuse for a country house, adds to the general sense of comical disappointment, frustration and futility that pervades *Tristram Shandy*. Details about Shandy Hall and its environs are surprisingly scarce, but what we do learn about it tells us a lot about the novel's characters and their preoccupations. It is likely that the first readers of *Tristram Shandy*, particularly if they frequented country houses themselves, would have been able to identify exactly who and what the Shandys were, where they came from, and the pretensions and frustrations that occupied their thoughts.

The Treasurer's House at York (Philip Halling)

Illustration of scene from *Tristram Shandy* by Hogarth

Shandy Hall (Gordon Hatton)

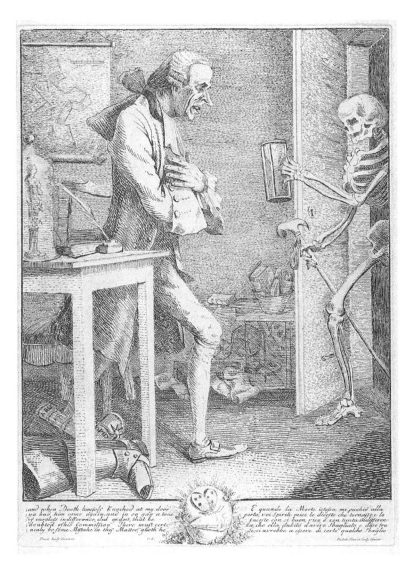

Tristram/Sterne confronts Death

York in 1782 (Wellcome)

John Locke

Toby and Mrs Wadman (Rijksmuseum)

Illustration for *A Sentimental Journey*

Ignatius Sancho (NY Metropolitan Museum)

IX. Tristram Shandy III: Walter

While the nature of the establishment at Shandy Hall gives us some clues about the background, mind-set and even the financial standing of Tristram's father Walter, other details in *Tristram Shandy* fill out the picture.

We learn that as well as ownership of the Hall, being head of the Shandy family brings with it certain other responsibilities, beside furnishing the parish with a bull. For one, he was obliged to pay an annual 'jointure' of one hundred and fifty pounds to his grandmother, which was provided for in the marriage contract between herself and his grandfather. Walter's mother would complain that this was an 'unconscionable jointure' to have to pay out of a 'small estate': was the estate bigger after Walter had made his mark in business? Certainly, the Shandys cannot have been paupers if they were able to pay this substantial sum every year.

Tristram explains that though his father would pay the hundred pounds (worth over twelve thousand today) with a good grace, the extra fifty found him looking 'at both sides of every guinea as he parted with it – and seldom could [he] get to the end of the fifty pounds, without pulling out his handkerchief, and wiping his temples' (TS III, XXXIII).

The reason why the Shandy estate has to continue to pay the 'unconscionable' jointure to the widow of Walter's grandfather, and for twelve years, is because this particular future Mrs Shandy insisted on extra money in her marriage contract, to make up for her bride-groom's diminutive nose. This is similar to the clause in Tristram's mother's marriage contract, where she stipulates that she should be allowed to spend the whole or part of any pregnancies in London, and not down at Shandy Hall. As we have seen, this is a way for Elizabeth to insulate herself from some of the possible bad effects of marrying a man who might at any point quit London and bury himself in the country.

Both Tristram's great-grandmother and also his mother insisted on certain clauses in their marriage-contracts to compensate themselves for the shortcomings of their bride-grooms. The great-grandfather had a short nose: but what is wrong with Tristram's father? As well as the likelihood that he will soon take up a country life, he must also be somewhat older than Tristram's mother Elizabeth, and he is also rather short in stature. We have already discovered that he is not a rich man, and he does not come from a particularly distinguished family: Tristram himself tells us that 'in all our numerous family, for these four generations, we count no more than one archbishop, a *Welch* judge, some three or four aldermen, and a single mountebank,' as well as a dozen sixteenth-century alchemists (*TS* VIII, III). Since by the eighteenth century it was widely suspected that the alchemists were never actually going to turn lead into gold or find a cure for death, the dozen sixteenth-century alchemists mentioned by Tristram may be yet another hint that the Shandys are cursed with a hereditary predisposition for disappointment and futility.

Linked, no doubt, to the comparative poverty of the Shandys of two generations above Tristram is the fact that Walter has not had the benefit of a university education. This becomes evident when he takes Tristram to enter his name at 'Jesus College ****': at this time the narrator's 'worthy tutor, and two or three fellows of that learned society' are astonished that such an eloquent man can be eloquent at all on the basis of such limited learning. Sterne is, however, too satirical to use this passage as an opportunity to praise what we now call higher education as such, and instead gives us an ambivalent picture of what Walter has somehow managed to do without:

he had never read *Cicero*, nor *Quintilian de Oratore*, nor *Isocrates*, nor *Aristotle*, nor *Longinus* amongst the antients; - nor *Vossius*, nor *Skioppius*, nor *Ramus*, nor *Farnaby* amongst the moderns; - and what is more astonishing, he had never in his whole life the least light or spark of subtilty struck into his mind, by one single lecture upon *Crackenthorp* or *Burgersdicius*, or any Dutch logician or commentator . . .

(*TS* I, XIX)

Tristram's list of authors his father has never read is a skilful mixture of well-known and obscure names. In the English context, it is half in and half out of the typical national attitude to education and academia in general: that it might be better left alone.

One consequence of Walter's mediocre educational background is the difficulty he has making sense of the obscure scholarly books in Latin that he acquires, though they are written about his favourite subjects.

The fact that Walter is able to enrol Tristram at a university is a hint that, even with his comparatively modest success as a merchant, he had raised the fortunes of the family sufficiently to pay for higher education for his second son. We also learn that he established Tristram's older brother Bobby at Westminster school: Bobby may not have benefited from higher education because he turned out to be 'a lad of wonderful slow parts' (*TS* II, XIX).

The marriage contracts mentioned in *Tristram Shandy* are a reminder that in those days women had very little wealth or power of their own, once they were married. A well thought-out marriage contract could, however, guarantee them certain rights throughout their marriage, and beyond. Tristram's great-grandmother continues to be paid her one hundred and fifty pounds per annum for the twelve years she remains a widow: the marriage-contract strategy therefore works for her. For Tristram's mother the Shandy family's tendency to step into quick-sands of disappointment and futility compromises her well-laid plan. After she has been taken all the way to London and found to have only a false pregnancy, she is too embarrassed to assert her rights in this respect ever again.

On this occasion, Walter is not only annoyed by the trouble and expense of the pointless trip to London: he is also disappointed that the second son he had hoped for is not yet forthcoming. This son he had begun to think of 'as a second staff for his old age, in case *Bobby* should fail him. The disappointment of this, he said, was ten times more to a wise man, than all the money which the journey, etc., had cost him' (*TS* I, XVI). Once again, disappointment and the sense of futility it brings with it.

The reason Walter has to continue to pay the jointure to his grandmother – his grandfather's stubby nose – connects to one of the great obsessions of Walter's life; the subject of noses. He firmly believes that great men have great noses, that everything possible should be done to ensure that one's sons have large noses, and that a small or short nose is a genuine curse. This is one of Walter's hobby-horses, and hobby-horses as such are an important ingredient in *Tristram Shandy*. Walter even attributes the low fortunes of the Shandy family in his own (short-nosed) grandfather's time to the deleterious effects of his grandfather's nose on the family's status and finances.

Walter's obsession with noses is set up by Sterne only to be knocked down by a classic comic catastrophe. When Dr Slop is called on to help out with Tristram's birth, he applies his impressive forceps only to crush the baby's nose.

We learn from *Tristram Shandy* that Walter was a 'Turkey merchant', meaning a member of the Levant Company, a chartered company set up by Elizabeth I in 1592. The company was supposed to have a monopoly of the British trade with the Ottoman Empire of the Turks: as such it exported British textiles, bullion and some other commodities, and imported Turkish silks, cottons and products such as dried fruit, leather, spices, drugs and chemicals.

To join the Company, which usually had around three hundred members at any one time, Walter Shandy would have had to pay a large up-front fee. He would then have been free to trade by exporting and importing goods he had bought wholesale, via the Company's ships. Many, including the Company's most distinguished representatives in Constantinople, made large fortunes in this trade and were thus able to banish any debts and restore the status of their families, if their families had got into debt and fallen on bad times.

There were also, however, ways to fail at the Turkey trade. Smaller traders had to accommodate themselves to the interests of the bigger traders within the company, who tended to have control over such matters as when the ships full of goods set out, and when they returned. Traders large and small were hit by factors such as shipwrecks, pirates and wars: wars in particular could shut down the trade for months on end. Even the grandest traders could also find their profits compromised by the notorious corruption of the Ottoman officials, who would impose arbitrary charges and restrictions, and otherwise harass and even lock up hapless Company men.

Competition from other European nations was a more or less constant threat to the viability of the Turkey trade, and in his history of the Company, Alfred Wood blames much of the steep decline in the Company's fortunes after 1718 on French competition. By the middle of the century, when Sterne was writing *Tristram Shandy*, the Levant Company was a shadow of its former self, and had become, in effect, obsolete.

Sterne's decision to make Walter Shandy a retired Turkey merchant fits well with many other ideas in *Tristram Shandy*. In many parts of the book, we get the feeling that Walter and Toby in particular are living in the past, clinging to outmoded notions and generally failing to live in their own part of their own century. The Turkey trade is just another bygone, like uncle Toby's outmoded costume. This sense of musty obsolescence is another factor that contributes to *Tristram Shandy*'s atmosphere of eccentricity, absurd comic disappointment and futility.

Walter Shandy, it seems, made no great name for himself among his fellow-members of the Levant company. He is determined, however, that his second son should at least start life with a great name, since he, Walter, believes that a good first name has as much of an effect on the success of a man as that other great obsession of his – a prominent nose. Still lamenting the injury to his as yet unnamed son's nose, Walter hears that his son has turned black and may die. This seems to be an instance of what is now called blue baby syndrome, the blueness being a symptom of poor oxygenation of the blood. Concerned that if the baby is dying it should be baptised first, Walter sends a servant with what he believes to be the greatest possible name, Trismegistus. Unfortunately the servant, Susannah, cannot keep the name intact in her head, and a curate (called Tristram) who is present baptises the baby Tristram; which of course Walter considers quite the worst name a boy could have (*TS* I, XIX). This accidental shortening of the intended name prefigures the later accidental shortening of Tristram's penis, or at least his foreskin.

Walter now has to lament his son's unfortunate conception, his nasal injury, and his dreadful Christian name. Later, he has to come to terms with the fact that his unfortunate Tristram has been circumcised by accident. The way that he copes with these crises is to deploy his considerable powers of eloquence, and to turn for succour to his small but curious library. The reader cannot help feeling, however, that all Walter's fine speechifying is merely evasion, and that he is unlikely to get any real help from a set of books dominated by obscure volumes on the subject of noses.

Walter's approach to the great events of life, at least in his retirement, is nicely demonstrated by his attempt to handle the delicate matter of the 'breeching' of Tristram. This was an important rite of passage for male children, the last vestiges of which did not entirely disappear even after breeches ceased to be acceptable as an item of modern menswear. Well into the twentieth century in England, the epoch-making change from short into long trousers was viewed by some as a step on the road to full manhood. Faced with this crisis, Walter turns to 'the ancients', who of course lived at a time when breeches had not been invented. They cannot help him; and the reader is reminded that, for all his eloquence, Tristram's father cannot actually hold a decent conversation with his own wife. They discuss the matter of Tristram's breeching one night in bed, but Elizabeth, Tristram's mother, kills this halting excuse for a conversation stone dead by simply agreeing with everything her husband says (*TS* VI, XVIII).

X. Tristram Shandy IV: Uncle Toby

Saddled with one 'slow' son and another who is unfortunate from birth, Walter Shandy also has to contend with a limited income and a turn of mind that sets him apart from most if not all other people in Christendom. He also has a young wife with whom he cannot communicate, and a gift for speech that cannot be lavished on an appropriate audience, and is not backed up by a sufficiently advanced education. He cannot genuinely share his eccentric interests with anyone: his frequent visitor, Parson Yorick, seems to view him from a considerable height, and with a wry smile. To cap it all, Walter's oldest son, the 'slow' Bobby, dies young.

Walter Shandy would seem like a pitiful, even tragic figure were it not for the great respect his son, the narrator Tristram Shandy, has for him; and the touching relationship he maintains with his near-neighbour and younger brother Captain Toby Shandy. I have already said that uncle Toby is 'perhaps the most attractive character in the entire canon of English Literature'. While Tristram respects the memory of his father, he practically worships the shade of his uncle, who possesses the qualities of loyalty and compassion to such an extent that the reader cannot help but love him.

Toby also has a fund of good old-fashioned common sense and plain religion, so that he is sometimes able to provide a counter-balance to his loquacious brother's wild speculations. When Walter is wondering how 'the mind is enabled to stand out, and bear itself up, as it does, against the impositions laid upon our nature,'

'Tis by the assistance of Almighty God, cried my uncle *Toby*, looking up, and pressing the palms of his hands close together – 'tis not from our own strength, brother *Shandy* – a centinel in a wooden centry-box might as well pretend to stand it out against a detachment of fifty men. - We are upheld by the grace and the assistance of the best of Beings' (*TS* IV, VII).

The fact that Toby drags 'a centinel in a wooden centry-box' into his plain, pious statement hints at his own hobby-horse – the obsession that makes him an unmistakably comic figure. Since he was injured during the second siege of Namur in 1695, Toby, together with his loyal servant Corporal Trim, has been building scale models of besieged cities. This began in Walter's house in London; but when Toby began to think that the table they were using there was too small, Trim had the bright idea of decamping to his master's modest country house and turning the bowling-green there into Namur in miniature. There Toby can sit in his own neat white sentry-box, no doubt feeling the same as a modern child does, playing with a train-set while wearing a train-driver's hat.

Like his brother Walter, Toby is a paradoxical character. Walter is a merchant with a longing for the life of a scholar: Toby is a soldier through and through, but he has none of the bitterness, harshness, callousness or drunkenness that we might expect from a military veteran who has witnessed some hard-fought battles. He never seems to laugh, true, but he is nevertheless a well of deep emotions, and can cry like a baby for the least reason.

If Toby and his servant Corporal Trim are supposed to be representative examples of veterans who fought at Namur, then one would think that the British army at that time was a host of angels in red coats. It seems, however, that this was not the case. This was the army that was re-built, for the benefit of the new King William III, from the shattered remnants of his predecessor James II's forces.

By the time it had been purged of the many Roman Catholics that James had inserted into the ranks, the British army was looking decidedly moth-eaten, especially since numbers had deserted or resigned because they felt they could not fight for William, since they had sworn to be loyal to James. Many also left the army by legitimate or illegitimate means because they did not want to perish in King William's wars on the Continent. As John Childs states in his book *The British Army of William III*, William invaded England and seized power partly so that he would have a British army to help him with his military projects. Because William's invasion of England put Protestant monarchs back on the English throne, many still refer to this event as the Glorious Revolution of 1688.

Childs also tells us that as long as his newly-acquired British army was usable, King William was not too concerned about the malpractice and corruption with which it was riddled from top to bottom. Officers nearly always bought their commissions, especially in peace-time, though King William hated the practice and tried to stamp it out. Sterne tells us that uncle Toby was 'born to nothing' except his commission, which suggests that what inheritance he had as a young man was used to buy him a place as a captain. This is similar to the way his older brother Walter would have tried to kick-start his own career by buying his own membership of the Levant Company.

Appointing army officers (or merchants) on the basis of their ability to pay for their positions is the opposite of meritocracy: at this time merit was much more central to recruitment and promotion in King William's Dutch army, which was one reason why he tended to look down on his British officers.

Under this informal system, it was likely that men who had used their own or their family's money to become, for instance, captains like Toby would try to abuse their new positions of power to recoup their original outlay, and even make money over and above their army pay. Childs has tales of officers claiming pay for soldiers who didn't exist, then persuading strangers, friends or servants to get into uniform and pretend to be soldiers when the troops were counted by visiting officials. These stand-ins were so widely-used that they even had a nick-name: they were called 'faggots'.

Other officers withheld pay, bonuses and bounties from their men, failed to supply them with adequate uniforms, weapons or other equipment, and insisted that local civilians furnish them with food and accommodation: this was the much-resented 'free quarter'. Some of these scams were necessary because army pay was seldom paid in full or on time.

It seems unlikely that honest uncle Toby would ever have employed such sharp practices: he may not have needed to in any case because, as well as his army pay of about one hundred and forty pounds a year, he also had an annuity, left to him by an uncle, of one hundred and twenty. Together these sums would amount to around twenty-eight thousand today.

Although he might not have defrauded his own country by such means as the use of 'faggots', Toby would certainly have suffered some of the consequences of widespread graft. He would have been fighting alongside ill-fed, unpaid, poorly-dressed and ill-equipped men whose bad experiences in the service might have made them more likely to desert, defect to the other side, disobey orders or just do as little as possible to contribute to the war-effort.

As the second son of a minor gentry family, who paid for his captain's commission, Toby Shandy would have been a fairly typical new recruit into King William's army after 1688. Tristram's uncle could not have bought his commission much later than that as we know that he was present at at least one of the sieges of the city of Limerick in Ireland: these took place in 1690 and 1691.

When the army was being boosted by new recruits at this time, to make up for the personnel it had lost during and after William's invasion, there were concerns that some very unsuitable types were buying commissions, including the sons of tradesmen, the tradesmen themselves, and even lawyers. Young gentlemen, whose incomes and families were considered unimpeachable, also bought commissions out of a misguided sense of adventure, though they had absolutely no military knowledge, training or experience.

The Nine Years War, in which the second seige of Namur was just one episode, was not the type of war Englishmen might sign up for out of a patriotic sense that without their help their country might be overrun by foreign invaders. For King William, the primary objective of this war was not even to force foreign troops out of some part of the British empire. As described by Childs, the new king's aim was to 'beat back the forces of Louis XIV and return the frontiers of the United Provinces to their position before the French invasion of 1672' (the United Provinces of the Netherlands was the predecessor of the modern Dutch state).

The British were forced to participate in this war: Childs calls its nine years a 'penance': 'nine long 'Hail Marys' imposed by the great father confessor of international relations'. Far from home, commanded by foreigners and despised by their new king, many of the British officers felt frustrated and impotent.

Toby was invalided out of the Nine Years War with what most men would think was the worst type of injury. Better to die with honour, some would say, or lose an arm or a leg, than be unable to father children. By now readers might have noticed that the male members of the Shandy family who feature most prominently in *Tristram Shandy* have something slightly embarrassing in common. This has to do with nothing else but their male members. Toby's may have been put out of action altogether at the second siege of Namur. Although Walter can use his, the last time he begets a child with it, things go horribly wrong. And poor little Tristram is circumcised by accident, and there is a hint that Dr Slop's treatment made the wound worse. Even the parish bull, owned by the Shandys, is not up to the job of impregnating the local cows.

Strange to say, infertility, impotence or misfortune in the business of begetting children was also a feature of the life of King William III, Toby's commander-in-chief at the second siege of Namur. His wife Queen Mary, through whom he claimed the English throne, miscarried early in their marriage, and never even conceived after that. And what did this Dutch king of England do while failing to beget children? He played at soldiers on the Continent; but with real soldiers, real weapons and in real countries, towns and cities. Is Sterne's uncle Toby's hobby-horse a satire on the reign of William III? Certainly Walter spots the potential for satire in his brother's hobby-horse. Reflecting on Toby's little white sentry-box, he says to Parson Yorick:

that if any mortal in the whole universe had done such a thing, except his brother *Toby*, it would have been looked upon by the world as one of the most refined satires upon the parade and prancing manner in which *Lewis* XIV. from the beginning of the war, but particularly that very year, had taken the field . . .

(*TS* VI, XXII)

But King Louis XIV of France had six legitimate children, and a number of illegitimate ones.

XI. Tristram Shandy V: The Female Characters

The second siege of Namur, in which Captain Toby Shandy was injured, was nevertheless considered a great victory for the Grand Alliance for which he was fighting. Such a victory was not to be enjoyed by uncle Toby when he laid siege to his attractive neighbour Mrs Wadman nearly twenty years later.

Like most of the other women in the novel, the widow Wadman is depicted as a very active character. Toby's attempt to woo her, which coincides with Corporal Trim's attempt to woo Mrs Wadman's maid Bridget, is really a kind of counter-siege: it was Mrs Wadman who set her cap at Toby first, made him notice her, and also began inquiries into the mysterious business of the nature of his injury. The initiative she shows is mirrored by the activity of the other leading female characters.

The female servants – the Shandys' Susannah and Mrs Wadman's Bridget, are forever acquiring and conveying current, crucial information; while Walter, Toby, Trim and indeed Tristram himself are in thrall to the charms of irrelevant, abstruse data about the minutiae of warfare, and what obscure renaissance, medieval and classical writers had to say about noses or costume. While the male characters tend to evade current events and concerns, the women are deeply involved; Mrs Shandy giving birth, and Mrs Wadman hunting down a new husband. When the male characters are active, their activity is comically futile: Toby and Trim endlessly build and re-build scale models of cities under siege, while Tristram's father spends hours writing his *Tristrapaedia*, a kind of syllabus for his second son's education, which can never be of any use because, while Walter is planning what his son should learn at a certain age, Tristram has already grown past that age.

As we have seen, for much of *Tristram Shandy* various male characters share the ground-floor parlour of Shandy Hall doing very little of any use, while Mrs Shandy, Susannah and the unnamed, traditional, female midwife are engaged upstairs in bringing a new life into the world. When Dr Slop, the male midwife, is invited to venture into the female preserve of the birth-room, the result is disastrous. His much-vaunted forceps, supposedly the latest in obstetrical instrumentation, crush the poor baby's nose.

Sterne's comically exaggerated picture of a household where the males waste time while the females are more active and useful is reminiscent of the way many homes were organised in England until quite recent times. Even in the nineteen-sixties, it was almost unknown for men to cook at home, and cleaning and laundry were complete mysteries to the average white British male. In those days, the excuse for men doing next to nothing in the home (or pursuing pointless hobbies) was that they were out at work all day, while their female partners often did no paid work at all. The Shandy men do not have this excuse: Toby and Walter are gentlemen, with private incomes.

The power of women as movers and shakers in *Tristram Shandy* manifests itself in Mrs Wadman as surprisingly overt sexuality. In a curious episode, we learn that, whereas the bottom of her night-shirt is usually pinned shut by her maid Bridget, when she begins to fall in love with Toby, she kicks up her feet and refuses to be pinned up in this way (*TS* VIII, IX). She uses the devastating tactic of getting Toby to look deep into her eye, to catch his attention, and she also employs Bridget to investigate Toby's wound as best she can, so as to avoid marrying an impotent man.

Mrs Wadman's pursuit of Toby, who seems to be quite unaware of her as a romantic prospect before she sets her cap at him, is reminiscent of the behaviour of school-children of a certain age in mixed-gender schools, where the girls generally become interested in the boys as potential sweethearts a little before the boys become interested in the girls in quite the same way. Uncle Toby's all-consuming interest in what is in effect an elaborate set of toys, from which Mrs Wadman has to distract him, adds to the adolescent flavour of aspects of Toby's response.

Sterne's frank depiction of Mrs Wadman's sexuality may just be his version of the old slander about widows being naturally highly-sexed and always on the lookout for a new husband or sexual partner. In the worst of unspoken traditions, they have often been labelled as a threat to marriages where the husband is still alive – one reason why widows sometimes lose friends shortly after they lose their husbands.

Insecure males have sometimes been concerned that a widow will compare their sexual performance to that of their late husband. This features in Henry Fielding's scandalous short novel *An Apology for the Life of Mrs. Shamela Andrews* (1741). After her wedding night, Shamela cannot help comparing her new husband to her previous lover, Parson Williams, and remarks, 'O what regard men who marry widows should have to the qualifications of their former husbands'. The term 'qualifications' is particularly pertinent to the case of uncle Toby and Mrs Wadman. With the assistance of her maid Bridget, she attempts an *examination* into Toby's physical condition, to try to ascertain if he is *qualified* for the married state.

The new looseness of Mrs Wadman's night attire is echoed in *Tristram Shandy* by the gaping skirt of Nannette, a peasant girl with whom Tristram dances during his visit to France. Sterne goes out of his way to make this scene seem like something from the ancient pastoral tradition of European literature:

A lame youth, whom *Apollo* had recompensed with a pipe, and to which he had added a tabourin of his own accord, ran sweetly over the prelude, as he sat upon the bank . . .

(*TS* VII, XLIII)

Tristram is invited to join in the dance, accompanied by the music of the lame youth and his sister, that the local 'swains' and 'nymphs' are enjoying at the end of their working day. Nannette, the narrator's dark-haired, 'nut-brown' dancing-partner, could hardly be more alluring, but Tristram is put out by the way that a split in her petticoat reveals her legs: 'I would have given a crown to have it sew'd up – *Nannette* would not have given a SOUS'. In response to Nannette 'capriciously' bending her head and dancing closer 'insidious', Tristram declares 'then 'tis time to dance off'.

In keeping with Sterne's determination to include his readers in his narrative, another sexually awake character in *Tristram Shandy* is the female reader. As he writes extensively and suggestively about noses, he warns this reader:

Now don't let Satan, my dear girl, in this chapter, take advantage of any one spot of rising ground to get astride of your imagination, if you can any ways help it . . .

(*TS* III, XXXVI)

It may be that Sterne intended his depiction of what we might call the superior sexuality of some of his female characters, and his 'dear girl' the female reader, as a general compliment to the female sex. Some critics have, however, followed this thread in *Tristram Shandy* to darker, more misogynistic aspects of Sterne's approach, and of his cultural background. Here female sexuality is sometimes depicted as threatening, out of control, and otherwise disgraceful. In an article included in the 2019 Norton critical edition of *Tristram Shandy*, Paula Loscocco, building on work by previous commentators, presents Walter Shandy in particular as a particularly nasty type of misogynist, viewing women as creatures of the flesh, while men are ruled by reason.

According to Loscocco, Walter Shandy is trying to construct a personal world where the dangerous influence of women is excluded, and pure masculine reason rules supreme. Certainly, it can be shown that neither of the Shandy brothers have much direct knowledge of or communication with women. In this context,

Loscocco points out that although Walter is supposed to be obsessed by the influence of a person's name on the life of that person, he never mentions any female names, and seems to assume from the moment of conception that his second child will be a son.

Loscocco's point of view may be a little extreme, especially for readers who see Walter in particular as a hapless rather than a threatening figure, but it does help us see extra significance in certain aspects of the novel. Is Walter's insistence that a male midwife be on hand during his wife's confinement an attempt to inject a male presence into the very female business of giving birth to a baby? Does Tristram's father see the supposedly more 'scientific' Dr Slop, with his published pamphlets on midwifery, as some kind of champion of the rational male principle?

Writers on *Tristram Shandy* often take what Sterne writes in the character of Tristram as a reflection of Sterne's own view. In the context of the gender politics of *Tristram Shandy*, this leads to concerns that Sterne himself may have been a misogynist, and that he was concerned to attack women in his novel. It may be that the novel is so complex and multi-layered that it will never be possible to state categorically that *Tristram* is a misogynistic text. Certainly the end result of Walter's insistence on the presence of Dr Slop during Tristram's birth does not tend to make the reader think that 'rational' man is of any use at all. Despite his theories, his training and his publications, Slop makes a mess of Tristram's birth, and later makes a mess of Tristram's penile injury. And what do his much-vaunted 'scientific' obstetrical instruments amount to? A 'crotchet' or hook, a 'squirt' and the forceps that crush little Tristram's nose.

XII. Dr Slop and Dr Burton

While on one level Sterne may have meant Dr Slop as a personification of (ultimately futile) male rationality and science, he may also have intended the character of the male midwife in *Tristram Shandy* as a satirical portrait of a real person; in this case, a Dr John Burton of York (readers may remember that an unnamed man-midwife also featured in the clueless Political Club in the 'key' to Sterne's *Political Romance*).

In literature, Sterne's period is particularly noted for its satire: the lives of the authors Alexander Pope, Jonathan Swift, Oliver Goldsmith, Henry Fielding and Joseph Addison all overlapped with the life of the author of *Tristram Shandy*, and all of them turned their hand to satire. Sometimes, as in Addison's Sir Roger de Coverley pieces, the satire is affectionate, and aimed at a species of people in general. At other times writers like Swift would aim carefully sharpened satires at government policies, as in the case of his *Modest Proposal.* Alexander Pope made enemies by cooking up elaborate satires and tipping them over the heads of specific people. In some cases, the satire's target seemed general, but at other times it was viciously specific.

Sterne undoubtedly had Doctor John Burton of York present in some part of his uniquely-structured mind when he was drawing the character of Dr Slop. Burton was indeed a male midwife or accoucheur, and, like Dr Slop, had published on medical subjects. Articles by Burton were brought out by the Edinburgh Philosophical Society in the 1730s, and his *Treatise of the Non-Naturals* was printed at York in 1738.

Sterne was by no means ignorant of the antiquated medical idea of the non-naturals, the subject of Burton's 1738 treatise. They are perhaps best defined as factors that are not directly connected to the human mind or body, but may influence the health of both. They include such things as good or bad air, and diet; but where Sterne mentions the non-naturals in *Tristram Shandy* he usually seems to be alluding to excretions, including semen. In a discussion of the various ways to describe a character, Sterne dismisses the idea of describing a man on the basis of his non-naturals, adding the remark, 'Why the most natural actions of a man's life should be called his Non-naturals, - is another question' (*TS* I, XXIII).

Walter Shandy believes that some regulation of his wife's non-naturals, during Tristram's gestation, might have undone the harm done by his disastrous conception; but he angrily states that Elizabeth's agitation about having a female midwife in attendance at the birth, and her frustration that she cannot live in London during her pregnancy, banish all her 'calmness and serenity of mind' and make 'due attention' to her non-naturals impossible (*TS* IV, XIX).

On the evidence of his *Treatise of the Non-Naturals*, Burton might have agreed with Tristram's father that Elizabeth's mood could have affected the development of the foetus: in one chapter of his treatise Burton writes about how the body is affected by the mind, though he admits that the reasons for these effects are little understood. In a very English way, Burton also employs many pages of his treatise in explaining how changes of weather effect peoples' health. He also warns against too much 'coition', as he calls it, and determines that of tea, coffee and chocolate (taken as a hot drink), the last is the healthiest.

Although Burton may have published his treatise as an elaborate kind of advertisement, reminding readers of his impressive college education obtained at Cambridge and Leiden, there is little to object to in his book, at least from the point of view of an eighteenth century reader who would not see, as we do, that its medical ideas are obsolete. By 1738 the author was established as a medic specialising in obstetrics in York, and the genteel population of that ancient city (who, as patients, were more likely to pay better) would have been impressed that their local accoucher was a published author.

The scholarly word 'treatise' is used in its title, but Burton's book was aimed not just at scholars, but at what we would now call the general reader. The author wanted to popularise his own ideas and those of the best medics of his time, particularly his Leiden professor Herman Boerhaave, a man possessed of 'a throng' of 'shining virtues and accomplishments', to whom he dedicated the book. Despite its bizarre talk of 'solids', 'fluids' and 'fibres', it is possible that some York hypochondriac, buying Burton's book in 1738, could have improved his health, especially if he paid attention to its old-fashioned insistence on moderation in all things.

A hard-working doctor/midwife who had written a useful book, and who had also founded the York County Infirmary in 1740: what was there in Dr Burton for Laurence Sterne to object to?

To begin with, the good doctor was a staunch Tory who worked hard to frustrate Sterne's uncle Jaques Sterne in his attempts to promote the Whig interest in York. Although Burton was actually living in Wakefield at the time of the 1734 general election, he made his presence felt in York, where the voting took place, by personally guarding a voting-booth. Even his York County Infirmary was a political tool; its backers, subscribers and founding doctors-in-chief being Tories. Its existence and its success allowed Burton to point out that the local Whigs had not supported it. The progress of the hospital was noted with approval by the aforementioned *York Courant*, the Tory paper that was led politically by Burton and his fellow medic Dr Drake.

In the hard-fought York election of 1741-2 Burton played a prominent part, accusing Jaques Sterne of threatening voters at Wheldrake that if they did not vote Whig, he would have part of their parish church demolished. But even though, as we have seen, Sterne's pen was engaged in that election, it was probably Burton's actions in 1745 that put him on the author's list of personalities worthy of a satirical roasting.

1745 was the year of the Jacobite Rebellion, remembered as 'the '45' for many years thereafter. As was the case with several wars, rebellions and other conflicts in Europe around this time, the Rebellion had to do with religion, and questions about the rightful successor to the post of monarch. As we have seen, the so-called Glorious Revolution of 1688 had removed the Roman Catholic King James II from the English throne and replaced him with the Protestant King William III. In the context of England in 1745, the Jacobites were the rebels who believed that James's successors should sit on the English throne. In '45, the rightful king, as far as the Jacobites were concerned, was James II's son, also called James, a Roman Catholic who regarded himself as King James III, and was sometimes called the Old Pretender.

It was James's son Charles Edward Stuart, remembered as the Young Pretender and Bonnie Prince Charlie, who led the revolt of '45. Starting from Scotland, where he had managed to capture Edinburgh, Charles entered England in November, with some five and a half thousand men at his back. The invading army got as far as Derby, where it turned back because the armed English Jacobites Charles had expected to join his force had failed to materialise in anything like the numbers he had hoped for. In April 1746 Charlie's army would be decisively defeated at Culloden, in what was to be the last pitched battle on British soil.

This all happened when Laurence Sterne was five years into his time playing the part of an obscure country parson, and the only piece of writing he may have produced in response to the Jacobite Rebellion was a stanza of six short lines that he contributed to a ballad written by his friend John Hall-Stevenson. As well as penning a ballad, Hall-Stevenson helped put together a small private army called the Royal Hunters, ready to face the Jacobite threat. Sterne attempted to persuade his servant Richard Greenwood to join a force such as Hall-Stevenson was involved with, but Greenwood refused and left Sterne's service. This was the same Richard Greenwood whose revelations about his old master's private life were published in *New Light on Sterne* in 1965.

Before Derby, the rebels had been at Lancaster where, for reasons that remain unclear, they were visited by Dr John Burton, the influential physician of York. Burton had ridden west, alone, across miles of country for his Jacobite rendezvous, and when he got to the city on the river Lune he was rewarded with an audience with the Young Pretender himself. Why he made the journey, and what exactly happened at Lancaster, are both mysterious.

Was Burton a secret Jacobite, or even a Catholic like Prince Charlie? Did he expect to stay with the rebel army? Did he think he might end up as the personal physician to the exiled King James III when he was restored to his kingdom? Did the rebels have a pressing need for an expert midwife? Did Burton return to York because he could tell that the rebels were never going to build up the numbers needed for success? Why was he given two valuable horses for his journey home? Is it possible that this struggling army could spare good horses? Was Burton a spy, and if so, whose side was he on? What did he expect to happen to him when he returned to York?

It seems that John Burton returned to York feeling confident that nobody would even question why he had met the rebels at Lancaster. When his old enemy Jaques Sterne suggested that he should be locked up, Burton laughed in his face. But Sterne's uncle was determined to exploit Burton's mistake, and he pushed hard to have the medic put away. As a result, the author of the *Treatise of the Non-Naturals* spent the winter of 1745-6 as a prisoner at York Castle, and was not released until 1747 when, despite Jaques Sterne's desperate efforts, it was found that there was not enough evidence to convict him of anything.

Writing *Tristram Shandy* in 1759, Sterne had evidently not forgotten Dr Burton: as Ian Campbell Ross points out, his satire against the York doctor becomes sharply focused during the scene where Corporal Trim reads out a sermon in the parlour of Shandy Hall (*TS* II, 9). The sermon is supposed to have been written by Yorick, the local parson, but in fact it is an old sermon written by Laurence Sterne himself, and given at the York assizes in 1750. Thanks to the decisions of the same assizes four years earlier, twenty-two men judged to have been Jacobite rebels were hanged, drawn and quartered. Jaques Sterne sat on the Special Commission that passed down these sentences.

The sermon examines the various ways that men interact with their own consciences, and with other factors that regulate their behaviour. The modern reader is likely to find little to object to in the sermon, until the author introduces a Roman Catholic as an example of a type of man who does wicked things, but hardly knows it because his religion keeps him in the dark:

his priest had got the keeping of his conscience; - and all he would let him know of it, was, That he must believe in the Pope; -go to Mass; - cross himself; -tell his beads; -be a good Catholic, and that this, in all conscience, was enough to carry him to heaven.

Not surprisingly, the Catholic Dr Slop goes to sleep during the sermon, and misses the part where the author mentions how 'the terrors of gaols and halters' help to keep men on the straight and narrow, even when their consciences and other considerations do not dissuade them from wrong-doing. Ross notices that Walter Shandy regrets how Dr Slop falls asleep 'before the time of his conviction,' a reference, perhaps, to Dr Burton of York, who could easily have ended up with his neck in a 'halter', meaning a hangman's noose, if things had gone differently.

After his mysterious trip to Lancaster and its anxious aftermath, John Burton was able to gradually climb back up to his former position of eminence in York society. He also tried to establish himself on the national stage by publishing his *Essay Towards a Complete System of Midwifery* in 1751. We can only imagine how he felt when he discovered that the nephew of his old enemy had put him in his book as a Catholic dwarf (in real life Burton was, by contrast, tall and well-made). Whether Burton deserved to have his old mistake of fourteen years earlier dredged up in this way is for the reader to decide. It may be that the Yorkshireman should have heeded his own advice, set out in the Preface to his *Treatise of the Non-Naturals* in 1738:

For whoever has been so hardy and refractory, as to detain the motives and reasons of their actions and behaviour from the world, have always found that the world would supply the deficiency, by forming ten times worse reasons, than the true ones would have been.

XIII. A Sentimental Journey

The reader of *Tristram Shandy* is tempted to think of Tristram as a sort of avatar of Sterne himself, though Yorick, the local parson who spends so much of his time at Shandy Hall, is closer to Sterne in many respects.

In the novel, Yorick lies somewhere between the most prominent characters, such as Walter and Toby, and smaller characters like Susannah and Obadiah. It is in Sterne's second novel, *A Sentimental Journey*, that Yorick takes centre-stage. It is unusual for a writer to pluck a character from one book and then make that character the dominant presence in a later work. Sterne would, however, have been aware that Homer did this: the epic poet of ancient Greece took the character of Odysseus from his *Iliad* and made him the eponymous hero of his *Odyssey*. Like Sterne's Parson Yorick, Odysseus stays in one place in the *Iliad*, whereas in the *Odyssey* Homer sends him on his travels: this is why the word 'odyssey' in English is a rather fanciful term for a journey, sometimes used ironically.

While Homer concentrates on the Greek hero Odysseus in his *Odyssey*, the Roman poet Virgil, writing centuries later, plucked the Trojan prince Aeneas from the Greek tradition and made him the hero of his *Aeneid*. Aeneas is also an unwilling traveller, who endures his own sometimes bitter odyssey. Virgil's hero mentioned by Sterne, writing as Yorick, in his *Sentimental Journey*. In the chapter called The Passport, Yorick tells us that he has often beaten off sadness and anxiety by forcing himself to experience substitute emotions, such as those that can be provoked by reading (he implies) the *Aeneid*. The passage where Aeneas meets the spirit of his spurned lover Dido in the underworld is one that seems to work in this way for Yorick: he remembers how he used to 'mourn for her [meaning Dido] when I was at school'.

In the *Aeneid*, Dido is the queen of Carthage in North Africa who kills herself after she has been seduced and then deserted by Aeneas. In France, Yorick encounters two melancholy women who might be intended as lightweight versions of Dido. One is the mysterious, sad, unnamed, brown-skinned lady Yorick encounters at Calais; the other is Maria of Moulines, a character recycled from *Tristram Shandy*, who roams, mad and beautiful, across the French countryside.

Both Aeneas in the *Aeneid* and Odysseus in the *Odyssey* encounter, and are tempted by, women. Both have opportunities to stay in foreign countries and live well with women who love them: Aeneas, notably, with the aforementioned Dido, and Odysseus with the nymph Calypso. Although its title makes it sound like a travel book, much of Sterne's *A Sentimental Journey* is taken up with accounts of encounters with women who tempt Yorick, and seem to be tempted by him.

Whereas Aeneas and Odysseus sleep with the women who tempt them, and then leave them, we assume that Yorick merely flirts with the women he encounters before continuing on his travels. Aeneas and Odysseus feel duty-bound to desert women like Dido and Calypso – Aeneas because he has some vast historic role awaiting him, and Odysseus because he has a wife and a kingdom waiting for him back in Ithaca. Yorick leaves his women behind because he feels it would be immoral to do anything else – he is, after all, a priest of the Church of England. In *A Sentimental Journey* he also repeatedly professes devotion to one Eliza, who is understood to be waiting for him at home like a kind of English Penelope. Either Sterne or Yorick have forgotten that Yorick is supposed to be married; or perhaps by this time he is a widower.

If we identify *A Sentimental Journey* with the *Odyssey* and the *Aeneid*, then we must identify *Tristram Shandy* with Homer's *Iliad*. Although an eccentric eighteenth-century comic novel cannot easily be compared to an ancient Greek epic, there certainly are similarities. There is a lot about war in Sterne's first novel – in particular, there is a great deal about walled cities under siege. Uncle Toby is of course wounded during the siege of a city, and most of the action of the *Iliad* happens during the Greeks' long siege of Troy. Partly because of its warlike character, the *Iliad* also has a very masculine atmosphere, which, as we have seen, is also the case in *Tristram Shandy*. There are also lengthy digressions in the *Iliad*, as Homer fills in what Holywood would call the 'back story' of his narrative.

It may seem fanciful to assume that Sterne was influenced by Homer and Virgil in this way, but for educated men of his generation the works of these ancient authors were central to culture and learning. Turning ancient epics to comic purposes was also a well-established practice – witness the *Dunciad* and *The Rape of the Lock* by Alexander Pope. Pope, who was born a quarter of a century earlier than Sterne, also made a respectable fortune from his verse translations of Homer. Sterne may also have drawn on his knowledge of Virgil's *Eclogues* and *Georgics* for the pastoral scenes in *Tristram Shandy* and *A Sentimental Journey*.

'Flirtation' may be too light a word to use for the encounters Yorick enjoys with women in *A Sentimental Journey*. Flirtation may be said to be based on the use of language, but when Yorick engages with a woman like the aforementioned lady at Calais, there is a great deal of what we would now call 'body-language', including touching, particularly of hands:

I fear in this interval, I must have made some slight efforts towards a closer compression of her hand, from a subtle sensation I felt in the palm of my own,—not as if she was going to withdraw hers—but as if she thought about it;—and I had infallibly lost it a second time, had not instinct more than reason directed me to the last resource in these dangers,—to hold it loosely, and in a manner as if I was every moment going to release it, of myself; so she let it continue . . .

This is all described with great subtlety and in exhaustive detail, so that whereas we might describe *Tristram Shandy* as a series of theatrical scenes, much of *A Sentimental Journey* appears like a film shot in ultra high definition, by a director with a penchant for extreme close-ups.

Yorick's eagerness for physical contact, however fleeting, with beautiful women may seem a little creepy, particularly in England in the twenty-first century when our traditional physical reserve is now coupled with more modern concerns about 'inappropriate touching' and the ways that the male touch can be used to emphasise the powerlessness of women. Yorick's use of the women he encounters on his travels, as sources of pleasurable *frissons*, can be seen as exploitative. The concern he sometimes seems to show for their own feelings and welfare may be just another sentimental indulgence: does he feel the same about long-dead Dido as he does about poor Maria of Moulines?

If the women he encounters find Yorick himself attractive, this may in part be due to his physical health. It is clear that he is not travelling for health reasons, as many of his contemporaries did (or pretended to do) but simply to gain experience of France and Italy. Unlike that other avatar of Sterne himself – Tristram Shandy – Yorick is not plagued with a 'vile cough'.

Yorick is quite aware that he should not be enjoying his intimate moments with strange women quite so much: he is successful in literally getting physically close to these women partly because he flatters them outrageously; a habit that also gets him into some glittering coteries in Paris. But it is all too much, and his conscience rebels against the results of his 'beggarly system' of flattering everybody:

The higher I got, the more was I forced upon my beggarly system;—the better the coterie,—the more children of Art;—I languish'd for those of Nature: and one night, after a most vile prostitution of myself to half a dozen different people, I grew sick,—went to bed;—order'd La Fleur to get me horses in the morning to set out for Italy.

Of course Yorick resolves to find children of Nature in Italy when there is only a tenth of his book left.

Despite his new resolve to abandon flattery, Yorick cannot abandon his sensual enjoyment of close non-sexual contact with melancholy beauties: in a few pages, he is feeding off the beauty and sorrow of the aforementioned Maria of Moulines like an emotional vampire.

The eloquence of expressions, gestures and physical movements is an idea that *A Sentimental Journey* inherits from *Tristram Shandy*. As in Sterne's first novel, the narrator breaks the fourth wall and tells us what he is thinking on such matters, referring to gestures and expressions as a form of short-hand:

There is not a secret so aiding to the progress of sociality, as to get master of this *short hand*, and to be quick in rendering the several turns of looks and limbs with all their inflections and delineations, into plain words. For my own part, by long habitude, I do it so mechanically, that, when I walk the streets of London, I go translating all the way; and have more than once stood behind in the circle, where not three words have been said, and have brought off twenty different dialogues with me, which I could have fairly wrote down and sworn to.

These reflections appear in the chapter called The Translation: Paris. They are written to expand on the effect of some polite gestures made by 'a kindly old French officer' with whom Yorick shares a box at the opera. The unnamed veteran puts Yorick in mind of 'Captain Tobias Shandy, the dearest of my flock and friends'; and Toby's older brother is also mentioned, in connection with obstetrics and the growth or otherwise of children. Tristram himself is mentioned in connection with the fantastical Maria of Moulines, whom he is supposed to have met on his own travels.

There may be an echo of Walter Shandy's character in one of the relatively self-contained stories Sterne injects into his *Sentimental Journey* (the self-contained story is another habit that is inherited from *Tristram Shandy*). In the chapter called The Sword: Rennes we learn about one Marquis d'E who, despite his high birth, lives to see his whole distinguished family sliding into poverty. He decides that there is 'no resource but commerce', but he places a symbolic old family sword in an ancient archive until he is rich enough to reclaim it and do it justice. If we think that the House of Shandy is as noble and ancient as the d'E tribe, then

Walter's attempt to restore its fortunes by trade via the Levant Company might be echoed by Yorick's tale of the sword.

At a little under forty-one thousand words, *A Sentimental Journey* is only about a fifth of the length of *Tristram Shandy*. Read in order of publication, it can serve as an after-dinner mint, light dessert or glass of French brandy after the huge feast of *Tristram*. Read in reverse order of publication, it can also work as an introduction or aperitif, since it can prepare the reader for many of the odd tricks Sterne employs in his earlier book. Most conspicuous among these is the sense that the narrator feels he has all the time in the world, so that although the book is called *A Sentimental Journey through France and Italy*, the novel is around one-fifth through before the action leaves Calais, and much of the rest of it takes place in Paris and Versailles.

The reader who undertakes to read *Tristram Shandy* closely followed by *A Sentimental Journey* may wonder why both novels contain accounts of Continental journeys. Is this lazy repetition, or is it a case of Sterne as author merely re-using his own real-life experiences of travel through France in particular? It may be so, but it must also be said that the journeys in the two books are very different, and though the travellers themselves – Tristram and Yorick – both share characteristics with their creator, they are different men, with different outlooks, and different reasons for travelling. Their journeys are also different in that whereas Yorick travels alone, Tristram takes members of his family with him.

Like *Tristram Shandy*, *A Sentimental Journey* opens with an interruption. When Yorick tries to persuade someone that 'they order . . . this matter better in France' his interlocutor breaks in with the natural question, 'You have been in France?' Like *Tristram*, Sterne's second novel ends with an eruption of something raw and physical into the narrative. In *Tristram*, this is the parish bull: in the case of *A Sentimental Journey*, the novel ends at the moment when Yorick's hand finally touches something other than a woman's hand, arm or leg.

XIV. Smollett, Locke, Aristotle's Masterpiece and Cervantes

Part of the reason why Sterne wrote *A Sentimental Journey* has to do with a non-fiction travel book of about the same length published by the Scotsman Tobias Smollett in 1766. Smollett's *Travels Through France and Italy* sold well for many years, and helped begin a popular trend for books of travels. Smollett himself appears in Sterne's *Sentimental Journey* as 'Smelfungus', in the early chapter called In the Street: Calais. Here we learn that, because of the 'spleen and jaundice' with which he set out, Smelfungus finds fault with everything on his Grand Tour. Smelfungus assures Yorick that he will tell the world about how badly he has been treated on his travels: 'You had better tell it, said [Yorick], to your physician'.

It is certainly true that Smollett's *Travels* contain many complaints from the author about how he was cheated, insulted and otherwise mistreated at every turn throughout his travels. It is also true that the author was very ill at the time: at one point, he abuses and threatens a whole mob of recalcitrant French people even though he can hardly breathe. He was almost certainly suffering from the same illness that afflicted both Sterne and Tristram Shandy, tuberculosis, though, as related in his *Travels*, Smollett cannot accept this even when one of the greatest authorities on lung diseases in Europe offers him the diagnosis.

One reason why Smollett mistrusted Dr Antoine Fizes' diagnosis was undoubtedly because Fizes, who was based at Montpellier, was a Frenchman. The Scotsman has little time for the

French, and describes them, in the pages of his *Travels*, as dirty, dishonest, frivolous, superstitious, lazy and lecherous, among other things, none of them good.

In *A Sentimental Journey*, Sterne contradicts Smollett's prejudice against this noble and ancient people, for instance by introducing the French version of uncle Toby, whom Yorick meets at the opera. Yorick's temporary servant, La Fleur, can also be seen as a youthful French version of the admirable Corporal Trim in *Tristram Shandy*.

Although, in his *Travels*, Smollett states that he admires some Frenchmen, almost everything he admires in France itself has little or nothing to do with the French as such. The French are not, of course, responsible for days of fine weather in the south of their country, or the noble remains of Roman architecture to be found in places like Nimes. In Rome, even Smollett's 'veneration for the antients' fails when he is disappointed by the Pantheon. As Sterne reports of Smelfungus in *A Sentimental Journey*, the Scotsman finds this remarkable building 'like a huge cockpit, open at the top'; 'no more than a plain unpierced cylinder, or circular wall' (Smollett's *Travels*, Letter 31).

In his *Travels*, Tobias Smollett does not hesitate to criticise and ridicule the Roman Catholic religion, features of which he naturally encounters throughout France and Italy. Perhaps because he wants to write a book that contradicts Smollett, Sterne abandons his own anti-Catholic feeling, which, as we have seen, is all too evident in *Tristram Shandy*, and introduces another admirable French character; the Franciscan monk who begs Yorick for a contribution at Calais. Sterne's hero manages to defeat his initial negative impression of the monk, but not before he has lectured him about how he would rather give his money to 'the lame, the blind, the aged and the infirm'. Yorick soon regrets his frosty lecture: it is implied that he would usually associate Franciscans with 'fat contented ignorance'; but the man's sad, wise look eventually wins him round, and they exchange snuff-boxes.

Although Sterne contradicted Smollett by praising many aspects of French life in *A Sentimental Journey*, some letters sent during his own travels in France reveal that he too found fault with, and could be exasperated by, much that he saw and experienced there.

The link between Sterne's *Sentimental Journey* and Smollett's *Travels* is self-evident and widely understood. The links between *Tristram Shandy* and Smollett's 1751 novel *Peregrine Pickle* are less well-known, but they are extremely striking and suggestive. As we have seen, these similarities were hinted at in an early anonymous review of *Tristram Shandy*, published in Smollett's magazine the *Critical Review* in January 1760.

Both the Shandys and the Pickles have comical surnames, and the fathers of both Tristram and Peregrine have retired to the country, having failed in business. In both novels, the heroes have eccentric uncles: Peregrine's uncle is to the navy what Tristram's uncle Toby is to the army: Commodore Trunnion lives in a castle he has, in effect, converted into a ship. Until he marries Peregrine's aunt, there are not even any beds in the place – only hammocks. Trunnion's fruity language is entirely nautical in character, and he has cannon in his garden, instead of the miniature cannon uncle Toby has installed on his bowling-green. The Commodore's servants are all ex-sailors who have served with the Commodore, much as Corporal Trim served with Toby.

The Commodore's marriage comes about because Peregrine's aunt sets her cap at the unsuspecting old sea-dog in much the same way that Mrs Wadman sets hers at uncle Toby. There is a great deal of action in Smollett's book before Peregrine is even born, and the hero's aunt becomes obsessed with her sister-in-law's condition while pregnant: she orders in books on obstetrics, and consults *Aristotle's Masterpiece*, of which more later.

In a possible echo of Sterne's *Political Romance*, where Trim the sexton goes to great lengths to bring a close-stool to the Parson, Peregrine's aunt moves heaven and earth to bring a particular chamber-pot to her pregnant sister-in-law. Peregrine's aunt has a false pregnancy, like Mrs Shandy, and a male midwife is called in to assist a traditional female midwife, who is first on the scene.

Whereas in *Tristram Shandy*, uncle Toby thanks his brother for going to the trouble of marrying in order to preserve the family name, in *Peregrine Pickle* the hero's aunt engineers her brother's marriage because she fears that the noble House of Pickle may peter out. Part of *Tristram Shandy* is concerned with Tristram's Grand Tour of the Continent, a type of trip that Peregrine also undertakes.

Whatever the relationship between Sterne's novels and the works of Tobias Smollett, part of his reason for writing *Tristram Shandy* was a desire to engage with the ideas of the English philosopher John Locke (1632-1704). Like both Sterne and Smollett, Locke suffered from lung problems; in his case perhaps a combination of bronchitis and asthma. Like both Smollett and Sterne, Locke also made the pilgrimage to Montpellier for the sake of his health.

Speaking to a French journalist called Jean-Baptiste Suard in Paris in 1762, Sterne is supposed to have implied that a careful reader would find the influence of Locke 'in all his pages, in all his lines, in all his expressions'. He also told Suard that Locke's was 'a sacred philosophy, without which' man will never 'attain to real command over nature'. As we have seen, when Sterne made the acquaintance of the French philosopher Denis Diderot in Paris, he made him a present of a number of English books: these included 'all Lock's works'.

Much of Locke's reputation as a philosopher rests on his book *An Essay Concerning Human Understanding*, which was published in its first form in 1689. In *Tristram Shandy*, the narrator summarises Locke's *Essay* as 'a history . . . of what passes in a man's own mind'. Locke begins his 'history' proper by proposing and defending his assertion that nothing 'of what passes in a man's mind' is there at birth: there are no innate ideas or principles; the mind of a new-born child is like a sheet of 'white paper, void of all characters, without any ideas': everything is acquired by experience.

Despite, or perhaps because of, Sterne's regard for Locke, much of *Tristram Shandy* can be seen as an attempt to prove Locke wrong, much as *A Sentimental Journey* tries to prove Smollett wrong in his ideas about France and the French. From the start, Tristram's mind is disordered by an unfortunate accident that occurs nine months before his birth. It is also clear that he has inherited the bad luck and eccentricity of his Shandy forbears.

It is hardly surprising, given that he regarded the mind of the new-born as a blank sheet of paper, that Locke also wrote about education, even in his *Essay*. Although he believes that many factors that come into play before birth are terribly important, Walter Shandy has a similarly high opinion of the importance of a good education. Unfortunately, his attempt to compile the aforementioned *Tristrapaedia*, a digest of everything he feels his son should know, proves as futile as much else he tries.

As well as Locke's idea of the mind of the new-born as a blank sheet of paper, Sterne makes use of Locke's examination of what he calls 'the association of ideas'. Locke begins chapter thirty-three of his *Essay*, which treats of this subject, by reminding his readers that people routinely 'observe something that seems odd . . . in the opinions, reasonings, and actions of other men'. This Locke ascribes to various causes, including the way people associate ideas that have no natural connection. As in the case of his idea that a child's mind is at first a complete blank, Locke considers the educational implications of his 'association of ideas'. He suggests that children should be carefully watched so that harmful associations are not planted in their heads: a 'foolish maid' might easily plant the idea that darkness is filled with 'goblins and sprites', for instance, and this must be harmful. Locke also warns that if a child's teachers are too harsh, he may never be able to enjoy books, and will always associate books and reading with pain and unhappiness.

In *Tristram Shandy*, Sterne links Locke and his association of ideas to his hero's unfortunate conception:

from an unhappy association of ideas, which have no connection in nature, it so fell out at length, that my poor mother could never hear the said clock wound up, - but the thoughts of some other things unavoidably popped into her head - and *vice versâ*: - Which strange combination of ideas, the sagacious *Locke*, who certainly understood the nature of these things better than most men, affirms to have produced more wry actions than all other sources of prejudice whatsoever.

(*TS* I, IV)

It is Elizabeth Shandy's mental association of sex with the winding up of a clock that leads to her disastrous question, 'Pray, my Dear, . . . have you not forgot to wind up the clock?'

Elsewhere in *Tristram Shandy*, odd associations of ideas are a symptom of the hobby-horses that obsess (we might say 'afflict') characters like uncle Toby and his older brother. Confronted by any kind of problem, Walter immediately plunges back into his curious books; and any word that has the remotest connection with anything military will set off uncle Toby's hobby-horse.

As well as his denial of innate ideas and his interest in the association of ideas, Sterne may have been influenced by Locke's approach to his readers in his *Essay*. The philosopher is forever explaining such things as why he wrote his book in the first place, anticipating objections his readers may have to his assertions, and apologising for passages that they might find problematic. He also asks his readers to recall examples of what he is writing about from their own experience. At one point, he tells the story of a man who cannot dance unless there is a trunk in the room, because there was always a trunk in the room where he learned to dance. In his conclusion to this odd story, Locke expresses some concern that the reader might suspect that he has dressed up the tale 'with some comical circumstances'. This the philosopher denies, and suggests, 'I dare say there are very few inquisitive persons who read this, who have not met with accounts, if not examples, of this nature, that may parallel, or at least justify this'.

While Sterne acknowledges his debt to Locke by mentioning the philosopher no less than six times in *Tristram Shandy*, he may have got his ideas about the harmful effects of an ill-managed conception such as Tristram's from a source that he mentions only once: *Aristotle's Masterpiece*. The reference comes during an argument between Walter and Toby, during which Walter accuses his brother of not knowing 'so much as the right end of a woman from the wrong' (*TS* II, VII).

If nothing else, a perusal of *Aristotle's Masterpiece*, with its anatomical diagrams and descriptions, might have enhanced Toby's knowledge in this area. This discussion of women's anatomy might have put the *Masterpiece* into Sterne's head, but he does not refer to any part of the book that deals with women's anatomy at all: he refers to the author's answer to the question, 'Why doth a man, when he museth or thinketh of things past, look towards the earth?'

Aristotle's Masterpiece was certainly not written by the ancient Greek philosopher Aristotle, but by an anonymous author, writing in English, late in the seventeenth century. It is a combined midwife's companion and sex-manual, among other things, and as such it thrived as a popular piece of 'underground' literature until well into the nineteenth century.

According to the author of the *Masterpiece*, which was published just five years before Locke's *Essay Concerning Human Understanding*, a terrifying number of factors can influence the future condition of a child before it is born. If the parents have sex too often or too seldom, if they are too young or too old, or if there is too great a discrepancy in their ages; if they have sex during the woman's period, if they are too excited about having sex – all these things can have a deleterious effect on the future child. The *Masterpiece* author is particularly keen to point out the severe effects of any thoughts that may cross the mother's mind during sex: if she is committing adultery, but thinks of her husband while she is doing it, for instance, the resulting child will look like her husband. Likewise, if she thinks about a black man during sex, the baby might be born black, though all of the child's grandparents and ancestors are white. By this reckoning, Tristram Shandy should have been born looking like a clock.

In the midwifery section of his book, the *Masterpiece* author insists that an expectant mother should be as serene as possible during the gestation of her child. Walter Shandy would certainly have agreed with this, and he is vexed that Elizabeth is herself vexed by the question of her spending her pregnancy in London, during Tristram's time in the womb. Walter himself would have been particularly interested in one piece of advice offered in

Aristotle's Masterpiece: the author asserts that if a child is born with a flat nose, this can be 'ascribed to the imagination of the mother, who has cast her eyes and mind upon some ill-shaped creature'.

We have already seen how in *Tristram Shandy* and *A Sentimental Journey* Sterne is forthright about women's sexuality – something that was widely denied and suppressed in the century after Sterne's. The *Masterpiece* author also recognises women's sexuality as a powerful force. When the 'natural purgations' of 'maids' 'begin to flow' their minds are stirred 'to venery'. If, at that point, a husband is denied them, they may become ill with 'the green weesel colonet, short-breathing, trembling of the heart, etc.' and may even 'break through modesty and satisfy themselves with unlawful embraces'. 'It is the same with brisk widows,' adds the *Masterpiece* author. The madness of Maria of Moulines, who appears in both *Tristram Shandy* and *A Sentimental Journey*, may be attributed to something like the sexual frustration that the *Masterpiece* author thinks should be avoided. We are told that she lost her reason when, for some reason, she was forbidden to marry by the local priest (*TS* IX, XXIV). Although he may not have been inspired by *Aristotle's Masterpiece*, Sterne's French friend Denis Diderot depicted the sexual frustration of a reluctant celibate in his novel *The Nun* (c. 1780).

Whether Sterne agreed or disagreed with Smollett, Locke or the *Masterpiece* author is probably irrelevant. His comic technique, particularly with regard to Locke, was to expose the revered philosopher's theories to light from a peculiar comic angle, to test out how they might apply to, and themselves illuminate, the ludicrous situations he creates. There is genuine bathos here: the sage philosopher is invoked when a man is comically interrupted during sex. Later, he is brought in when a foolish thought about a night-gown enters the head of a maid sitting in the kitchen at Shandy Hall (*TS* V, VII).

Smollett, Locke and the *Masterpiece* author are by no means the only writers Sterne drew on or referred to as he was writing *Tristram Shandy*. Indeed whole books have been written on the subject, one of the most influential being John Ferriar's

Illustrations of Sterne, published with other material from Ferriar in 1798. Ferriar revealed that Sterne had borrowed so much from such works as Robert Burton's *Anatomy of Melancholy* (published in its first form in 1621) that when H.D. Traill gave an account of Ferriar's work in his 1901 biography of Sterne, he had to include it in a chapter sub-titled 'The Charge of Plagiarism'. Ferriar also examined Sterne's debt to Francis Bacon, Cervantes, Shakespeare, Addison, Michel de Montaigne, François Rabelais, Jonathan Swift and a number of less well-known authors.

To pluck just one name from the list above, Miguel de Cervantes, who died in 1616 (the same year as Shakespeare) wrote *Don Quixote*, one of the most influential works in the western tradition. As a comic novelist, Sterne evidently felt that he owed a debt to the great Spaniard: he mentions Cervantes six times in *Tristram Shandy*, using the adjective 'Cervantick' three times.

Perhaps the most Cervantick element in *Tristram* is the relationship between Corporal Trim and uncle Toby. Although Trim is technically Toby's servant, it is clear that he is also what we could now call the old captain's 'carer'. By a subtle mix of gently suppressing, but at the same time humouring, Toby's behaviour, Trim helps his eccentric master to live something like a normal life. This is surely inspired by the relationship between Don Quixote and his servant Sancho Panza in Cervantes' masterpiece. Like Trim, Sancho shares some of his master's delusions, but his solid peasant good sense saves the crazy old man from even worse calamities than those he endures.

XV. Ignatius Sancho and Sterne's Sermons

The Cervantick Laurence Sterne had a friend called Sancho: this was a remarkable Londoner by the name of Ignatius Sancho. Sancho was born around 1729 on a slave-ship plying the notorious middle passage, in this case between Africa and the Spanish colony of New Grenada. His mother died, probably as Sterne's father had in Jamaica, of the 'country fever' shortly after Sancho's birth, and his father committed suicide rather than live as a slave. A bishop in the Spanish colony baptised the child with the name of Ignatius, and his master took him, aged about two, to Greenwich. There three unmarried sisters adopted him and gave him the surname Sancho, in recognition of his obesity. In *Don Quixote*, Sancho Panza's barrel-like shape contrasts with the mad knight's pitiful leanness.

The three maiden sisters of Greenwich denied Sancho a proper education, but the boy was taken in hand by John, the second duke of Montagu, who found him very intelligent, lent him books and encouraged his reading. After the duke's death, Sancho ended up working as butler in the household of his widow. On her death, he came into a year's salary and a pension worth thirty pounds a year. Later he became valet to another Montagu, but his obesity and gout forced him to open a grocery shop in Westminster, with his wife Anne. Sancho supplemented their income by writing plays, musical compositions and newspaper articles. He was also a superb letter-writer, and in 1782 a posthumous edition of his letters, prefaced with a short biography, proved a surprise bestseller, bringing his widow a windfall equivalent to over forty thousand pounds at twenty-first century values.

Sancho first wrote to Laurence Sterne in July 1766, prompted by a passage in one of his correspondent's sermons. Sermons written by Sterne had been published before, but after the success of the first volumes of *Tristram Shandy* a selection was published in two volumes in 1760, under the title *The Sermons of Mr Yorick*. The passage that had caught Ignatius Sancho's eye is in a sermon with the cumbersome title *Job's Account of the Shortness and Troubles of Life, Considered*. Here Sterne paints a melancholy picture of the shortness and troubles of life, inspired by a familiar text from the Old Testament book of Job; 'Man that is born of a woman, is of few days, and full of trouble:— He cometh forth like a flower, and is cut down; he fleeth also as a shadow, and continueth not'. The text will be familiar to many readers because it is used in some Christian funeral services.

It is clear from Sterne's sermon that life in eighteenth century England was indeed shorter and more troubled than it is today. High infant mortality was a heart-breaking fact of life, and Sterne mentions 'the newborn babe' who 'falls down an easy prey, and moulders back again into dust'. Infant mortality combined with other factors to ensure that, as Sterne asserts, half of all the people born in those days died before they were seventeen years old.

Another of the evils of his day that Sterne mentions is slavery; and this is the passage that prompted Ignatius Sancho's letter: 'Consider slavery—— what it is,—— how bitter a draught, and how many millions have been made to drink of it'.

'Your Sermons have touch'd me to the heart,' wrote Sancho, 'and I hope have amended it, which brings me to the point . . . I am sure you will applaud me for beseeching you to give one half hour's attention to slavery, as it is at this day practised in our West Indies.—That subject, handled in your striking manner, would ease the yoke (perhaps) of many—but if only of one—Gracious God! - what a feast to a benevolent heart!'

It looks like Sancho put a lot of thought into his letter, fine-tuning it so that it would appeal to its famous recipient and elicit a positive response. He shows himself to be a fan of Sterne's writings, and a man of culture, by praising the characters of uncle Toby and Corporal Trim in *Tristram Shandy*. He also shows himself to be a man of sentiment by telling Sterne how much an 'affecting passage' in his sermon has moved him. The passage 'has drawn a tear in favour of my miserable black brethren', and Sancho suggests that Sterne's own response will be 'a feast to a benevolent heart', since Sterne is, according to Sancho, 'an epicurean in acts of charity'. In this way, Sancho is making an emotional appeal – trying to find common ground between himself and his correspondent in the area of their emotions, or sentiments: 'you cannot refuse,' he insists; 'Humanity must comply'.

Sterne replied from Coxwold less than a week later, in a style that must have reassured Sancho that he had successfully worked on the emotions of at least one man of sentiment. Sterne reported that he had just 'been writing a tender tale of the sorrows of a friendless poor negro-girl'. The writing of the passage, which probably has something to do with a scene that appears in the sixth chapter of book nine of *Tristram* had, he admits to Sancho, made his eyes smart. The 'poor negro-girl' works in a butcher's shop in Lisbon, where Trim's brother Tom sees her working at shooing away flies 'with a bunch of white feathers slightly tied to the end of a long cane'. She does not kill the flies because, as Toby suggests, 'she had suffered persecution, *Trim*, and had learnt mercy'.

'If I can weave the Tale I have wrote into the Work I'm [about]', wrote Sterne to Sancho, ''tis at the service of the afflicted —and a much greater matter; for in serious truth, it casts a sad Shade upon the World, That so great a part of it, are and have been so long bound in chains of darkness & in Chains of Misery'.

The passage about the 'poor negro-girl' in *Tristram Shandy* is part of Trim's account of his brother, who, at the time of Tristram's birth, has long been in prison in Portugal, at the mercy of the Inquisition. As if Sterne habitually associated slavery with prison and Roman Catholicism, his Job sermon quickly moves from the lament over slavery that had so moved Ignatius Sancho to a bitter condemnation of the Inquisition and 'the Romish church' in general. 'Examine the prisons of the inquisition,' Sterne writes:

'hear the melancholy notes sounded in every cell'. These are to be blamed on 'the Romish church and her tyrants' who are responsible for 'both the slavery of body and mind': the prisoners suffer there because 'a false and a bloody religion has condemned them'.

The way that Sterne's anti-Catholic feeling breaks out here rather spoils the enlightened and enlightening effect of the author's condemnation of slavery. When, in his reply to Sancho, he branches out into a consideration of how many people 'have been so long bound in chains of darkness & in Chains of Misery', one cannot help thinking of the poor Roman Catholics of England, and especially of Sterne's native Ireland, who suffered so much hardship, and so many legal and social disadvantages, simply because of their religion.

It is hardly surprising that a passage in his Job sermon drew a tear from Ignatius Sancho's eye. In keeping with his status as a master of sentiment, Sterne often seems to be trying to wring his readers' (or listeners') hearts, in his sermons as well as in his fiction. In his sermon on the Levite and the Concubine, based on Judges XIX, 1-3, he practically excuses the Levite (a Jewish priest) for having a concubine, meaning a type of mistress, on the basis of the emotions their tale is likely to elicit in a sentimental heart. In the sermon, which was published in 1766, the couple are described as 'a most sentimental group'; only '*spleen* or *prudery*' will make the picture seem dirty. *Candour* and *courtesy* will be kinder: 'Nature will have her yearnings for society and friendship . . . let the torpid Monk seek heaven comfortless and alone' (note that even here Sterne manages to criticise the Roman Catholic Church: he is surely not thinking about an Orthodox Christian monk).

It is tempting to speculate on the effect Sterne's Levite sermon had on its fist hearers, especially if those hearers were aware of the rumours that this particular preacher had himself not endured the period before his marriage 'comfortless and alone' like a 'torpid Monk'. Depending on exactly when the sermon was first preached, the congregation may also have been able to reflect that their own Christian Levite had not been as loyal and loving to his lawful wife as the Levite in the story is to his concubine.

It is likely that many in Sterne's congregation would not, however, have understood enough of his Levite sermon to have been able to apply it to what they knew of the private life of the preacher. As S.C. Carpenter reminds us in his book *Eighteenth Century Church and People*, many of the sermons preached in Sterne's day would have gone right over the heads of the typical church-goer. In the Levite sermon, Sterne quotes passages from scripture without telling us where the quotations come from, something that would have made many of his listeners feel excluded. He also assumes that his hearers are already familiar with such Biblical characters as Hagar, Rachael, Leah and Rehoboam, and uses hard words like 'intercourses', 'patriarchs', 'dispensation' and 'reproachable'. In Sterne's century, the Methodists were among those who pioneered the use of sermons that ordinary people could actually understand. For John Wesley in particular, the revelation that many ordinary people knew next to nothing about the basic Christian message forced him to change his approach.

Sterne does not name any specific non-Anglican Protestant sects in his sermon On Enthusiasm (published in 1769) in which he warns against the 'violent extremes' that led to 'the great and unedifying rout made about sanctification and regeneration in the middle of the last century, — and the enthusiastic extravagancies into which the communications of the spirit have been carried by so many deluded or deluding people in this'. Like a true representative of the state church, he recommends a view of Christianity 'as the most rational, sober and consistent institution that could have been given to the sons of men'. Sterne's On Enthusiasm is a sermon that was particularly likely to have flown right over the heads of the author's unlettered listeners. Here he quotes the Roman author Seneca in the original Latin, writes very long, involved sentences, and uses such words as 'inference', 'sufficiency' and 'unintelligible'. Never one to miss a chance to kick the Roman Catholic Church, Sterne suggests that people who are afflicted with too much religious enthusiasm are so wrong-headed that they are almost bound to turn to Rome, 'after which I cannot see how they can possibly refrain going to mass, consistent with their own principles'.

In his sermon On Penances, also published posthumously, Sterne names the Methodists and criticises what he perceived as the gloominess of their approach. 'The Author of our religion,' he asserts, has not 'created us on purpose to go mourning, all our lives long, in sack-cloth and ashes' and, reminding us of Don Quixote, Sterne suggests that the Creator did not send us 'into the world, as so many saint-errants, in quest of adventures full of sorrow and affliction'.

In its talk of '*spleen* and *prudery*' Sterne's Levite sermon criticises gossip and scandal-mongering. These were definitively lambasted in Sheridan's play *The School for Scandal* (1777) where the idea of the 'man of sentiment' also came in for criticism. The aptly-named Joseph Surface, a character in the play, is praised for his virtue and his tender feelings, but is ultimately exposed as a hypocrite. Sterne's sentimentality has often been criticised on purely aesthetic grounds: is it not sometimes overdone and mawkish? Is there not a sense that the author is trying to extract the maximum of emotion from an idea or situation, and failing to see or depict the situation accurately, as he views it through eyes made bleary with tears?

For some of Sterne's generation, tearfulness may have been part of an appropriate response to the horrors of slavery, but merely emoting about the tragic trade was never going to be enough, any more than Yorick's tearful distribution of a few coins to the destitute of Calais in *A Sentimental Journey* was going to solve anything long-term. A saying of the Brazilian archbishop Hélder Câmara (1909-1999) might be worth quoting here: 'When I give food to the poor, they call me a saint. When I ask why they are poor, they call me a communist'.

In his introduction to the first, 1760, edition of his sermons, Sterne asserts 'that not one of them was composed with any thoughts of being printed' and that 'they have been hastily wrote, and carry the marks of it along with them'. Later the author suggests that 'the reader, upon old and beaten subjects, must not look for many new thoughts' and admits that, like Homenas in the *Rabelaisian Fragment*, he has 'taken the same liberty' of borrowing from other authors without acknowledgement.

In his biography of Sterne, H.D. Traill goes rather further than Sterne himself in criticising his own sermons. The 1760 volumes are, to Traill, 'the chance sweepings of the parson's sermon-drawer', 'of the most commonplace character; platitudinous with the platitudes of a thousand pulpits, and insipid with the *crambe repetita* of a hundred thousand homilies'.

Despite their faults, the sermons of Mr Yorick proved very popular in 1760: as we have seen, more were published in 1766, and in 1769, after Sterne's death.

The publication and reading of sermons had pretty much died out by the end of the twentieth century, although in the middle of the eighteenth century an average of over sixty books of sermons were published every year. In the twenty-first century, sermons are regularly published by other means: the 'sweepings of the parson's sermon-drawer' can now be e-mailed to parishioners, put up on parish or diocesan websites, and shared via social media.

XVI. The Journal to Eliza

Throughout *Tristram Shandy*, the narrator invokes the name of Jenny, his mysterious mistress, mentioning her fifteen times. Yorick, the narrator of *A Sentimental Journey*, mentions his Eliza six times. The identity of Eliza is not at all mysterious: it is not Sterne's wife Elizabeth, but a much younger woman, also married, called Eliza Draper. Although, as we have seen, the Yorick of *A Sentimental Journey* does not seem to have Sterne's cough, he does have a sweeter affliction – his author's love for Mrs Draper.

Eliza Sclater had been born at Anjengo (now Anchuthengu in the Indian state of Kerala) in 1744. At the age of fourteen she had married Daniel Draper, an official in the East India Company, the company that rivalled Walter Shandy's more old-fashioned Levant Company at this time. The marriage was not a success: Draper was known to have mistresses of both Indian and European descent, and Eliza ran away from him in 1773, returning to England in the next year. By then Sterne had been dead for some time.

Eliza spent much of her life in India, but for part of 1765, the whole of 1766 and the first months of 1767, she was in England. She probably met Sterne for the first time early in 1767, at the house of their mutual friends, Commodore Sir William James and his wife Anne, who lived in Gerrard Street, Soho, close to Sterne's London lodgings at Old-Bond Street. At the time of writing, Gerrard Street is part of London's thriving Chinatown.

Sterne was quickly captivated by Eliza, as much of London had been. They called her the *Belle Indian*, although even Sterne admitted that she was not what we would now call a conventional beauty: it was her fine eyes and her witty conversation that made her so appealing. What attracted the youthful Mrs Draper to Sterne, a married, consumptive clergyman in his mid-fifties, is less clear. He was certainly one of the literary lions of the age, and his conversation was no doubt captivating, and his attentions flattering, but it seems likely that Eliza was not as physically attracted to him as he was to her. Something they did have in common, which may have helped the friendship along, was that they were both children of Britain's burgeoning empire, English by ethnicity but not by birth, born in places where a few Brits lorded it over thousands of down-trodden natives.

Before Mrs Draper returned to India in April 1767 she and Sterne agreed that they would each keep a journal in which they would write to each other on a regular basis. Although they might also send 'proper' letters to each other, which would be sent off in the usual way, they would only share the journals when they were reunited. In recognition of Eliza's Indian origin, he calls her his 'Bramine', and she calls him his 'Bramin'.

Of course the reunion Sterne longed for in his *Journal* never happened; but its pages are full of his fantastic plans for their reunion. He calls her his wife, and at one point he writes as if he were some future 'annotator or explainer of my works', looking back at their ideal life together:

Mr. Draper dying in the Year * * * * * This Lady return'd to England & Yorick the Year after becoming a Widower—They were married—& retiring to one of his Livings in Yorkshire, where was a most romantic Situation—they lived & died happily—and are spoke of with honour in the parish to this day

Because of the impossibility of divorce for people like Sterne and his Eliza at the time, the author's deluded plan depended on the early deaths of both his own wife and Eliza's husband. In the event, both Mr Draper and Mrs Sterne outlived the real-life 'Yorick'. Sterne should have expected this: the *Journal to Eliza* is full of accounts of the alarming symptoms of his by now advanced tuberculosis, and of the sometimes equally alarming treatments prescribed for him. He is confined to bed for long periods, but his rest is constantly interrupted by visitors '& my rapper eternally going with cards and enquiries after me'. The 'cards' were of course the polite visiting-cards that were much used at this time.

Among his visitors were his doctors who, the *Journal* tells us, were convinced that his was a 'venereal' case, meaning that they thought he had a sexually transmitted disease. They probably thought Sterne had syphilis, since they prescribed 'a course of mercury', but Sterne protested ''tis impossible . . . for I have had no commerce whatever with the Sex—not even with my wife, added I, these 15 years'. If true, this would suggest that Sterne had been celibate since around 1752, five years after Lydia was born and ten years into his long stint as a country parson. What could have stopped Laurence's enthusiastic philandering, which may once have seen him running after York prostitutes and his own servants? It may be that he had been diagnosed with a sexually transmitted disease back then, but had hoped that by 1767 it had worked its way out of his system.

The doctors also tried bleeding the author: at one point his bandages came loose after a bleeding session and he nearly bled to death in his sleep. When he was better, he was able to spend time at Coxwold, and at his friend John Hall-Stevenson's Crazy Castle, where he enjoyed participating in carriage-races along the nearby beach, but cut short his stay because there was too much 'company and dissipation'. At Coxwold, he imagined he saw Eliza everywhere, and he said that the improvements he mas making to the house were all for her:

I have made you a sweet Sitting Room (as I told You) already—and am projecting a good Bed-Chamber adjoining it, with a pretty dressing room for You, which connects them together—& when they are finish'd, will be as sweet a set of romantic apartments, as You ever beheld . . .

Although some of the details in the *Journal*, particularly the suggestion that its author might have syphilis, seem calculated to put Eliza off her Yorick, his descriptions of his life and his house at Coxwold are more inviting, though it is possible that, following her success in London, Eliza would have preferred to live with Sterne in the capital.

In the *Journal*, Coxwold is 'a delicious retreat' where the author lives in a 'princely' manner, sitting down to:

Venison, fish or wild foul—or a couple of fouls—with curds, and strawberrys & cream, (and all the simple clean plenty which a rich Vally can produce,—with a Bottle of wine on my right hand (as in Bond street) to drink your health—I have a hundred hens & chickens about my yard—and not a parishioner catches a hare a rabbit or a Trout—but he brings it as an offering—In short 'tis a golden Vally—& will be the golden Age when You govern the rural feast, my Bramine, & are the Mistress of my table & spread it with elegancy and that natural grace & bounty with which heaven has distinguish'd You …

An eighteenth-century reader, perusing the passage above, might suspect that the 'parishioner' who brought some of his catch to the parsonage was in fact a poacher, and that the wine at Sterne's right hand was smuggled: the proceeds of these illegal activities were often shared with figures of authority such as the local parson, in the hope that they might turn a blind eye.

While enjoying the 'golden valley' at Coxwold and writing his *Sentimental Journey* and the *Journal to Eliza*, Sterne dreaded the projected visit of his wife, who, he assured Mrs Draper, was only coming so that she could agree the details of her financial future with her husband. She was determined to stay in France for the sake of her health: in the *Journal*, Sterne seems to regard her upcoming visit as a last painful encounter he has to endure in order to be rid of her.

Whatever Eliza Draper herself thought about Sterne's devotion, she would probably have thought less of it if she had known that her friend had enjoyed a similar relationship with another young lady just before he became famous as the author of *Tristram Shandy*. Laurence met the singer Catherine Fourmantel in 1759, when she was in York fulfilling a professional engagement at the city's Assembly Rooms. Their first meeting must have been around the time when the Sternes moved from Sutton to a house in

York's Mint Yard. They met, wrote to each other and exchanged gifts, and Sterne called her 'my dear Kitty' and 'my dear dear girl'. As in the case of his Eliza, Sterne seemed to think that there was a chance that he could marry his 'Kitty', if only his wife would do them the favour of dying. But the author's interest in his singer quickly faded as he became the most celebrated novelist in England.

Catherine was not the only female with whom the author carried on a serious flirtation: in fact he always seems to have had some woman or women to whom he was writing sentimental letters, and with whom he was having incautious meetings. The identity of some of these women remains a mystery, and it is still unclear whether Sterne actually managed to get into bed with any of them.

Older editions and biographies of Sterne do not mention his *Journal to Eliza:* the *Journal* did not come to light until the middle on the nineteenth century, when Thomas Washbourne Gibbs, a gentleman of Bath, revealed that he had it in his possession, together with other important papers relating to Sterne. Gibbs had known about these papers since he had inherited them from his father during his childhood. How his father got them remains a mystery.

In 1851, Gibbs sent the papers to the author William Makepeace Thackeray, who was then writing his book *English Humorists of the Eighteenth Century*. Although Thackeray, the author of *Vanity Fair* and *Barry Lyndon*, did not quote directly from the *Journal* in his *English Humorists*, it is likely that he had at least looked over it, together with Gibbs' other Sterne papers, before he wrote what amounts to a vicious attack on Sterne in that book. Later, in 1878, Gibbs read a lecture about his Sterne papers to the Bath Literary Institution: the substance of this lecture was printed in *The Athenæum*, a literary magazine, in the same year. When Gibbs died in 1894, his papers passed to the British Museum, but they were not published until 1904. In the next year, copies of the original printed version of Sterne's *Political Romance* were rediscovered.

If we view Sterne's *Journal to Eliza*, *Sentimental Journey* and *Tristram Shandy* together, it appears remarkable, the extent to which these works refuse to stand alone: they bleed into each other and into Sterne's own life and letters, and even into his sermons. As we have seen, a sermon of Sterne's is included in *Tristram Shandy*, and the whole of *A Sentimental Journey* centres on a character taken from the earlier novel. Tristram, uncle Toby and Walter Shandy are all mentioned in *A Sentimental Journey*, and Yorick's Grand Tour echoes the earlier one taken by the Shandys. As we have seen, Yorick even meets Maria of Moulines, who features in *Tristram Shandy*. Sterne mentions Tristram in the *Journal to Eliza*, calls himself Yorick, and mentions how he is progressing with the *Journey*.

It is clear from Sterne's *Journal to Eliza* that without exceptional medical treatment and a large dose of good luck the author was not likely to live much longer. In fact, he lasted for less than a year after Eliza left for India, dying in London on the eighteenth of March 1768.

By sheer luck we have a calm, circumstantial account of Sterne's last moments from one John Macdonald, a footman employed by the author's Scottish friend John Crauford. Crauford was dining that Friday afternoon at a fine house he had taken in Clifford Street: among his guests were the actor David Garrick and the philosopher David Hume. Crauford turned to his footman and said, 'John . . . go and inquire how Mr Sterne is today'.

In *Memoirs of an Eighteenth Century Footman* Macdonald tells us that he arrived at Sterne's lodgings just five minutes before the end. 'Now it is come,' said the dying man: Macdonald continues 'he put up his hand as if to stop a blow, and died in a minute. The gentlemen were all very sorry, and lamented him very much'.

The Shakespearian scholar Edmond Malone, who is also a source for the story of the theft of Sterne's body, wrote that 'the celebrated writer Sterne, after being long the idol of this town, died in a mean lodging without a single friend who felt interest in his fate'. This may be a little melodramatic, and in any case Sterne, writing as Tristram Shandy, stated a preference for not dying at home, 'but rather in some decent inn' where 'the few cold offices I wanted, would be purchased with a few guineas, and paid me with an undisturbed, but punctual attention' (TS 7, 12). This kind of death, Tristram implies, would mean less distress for his friends and relatives (who would of course be absent) and therefore for himself.

In the *Life of Edmond Malone* by James Prior we learn that Malone said the only friend who attended Sterne's burial was the bookseller Thomas Becket. Ross insists that there were 'two or three mourners' in attendance when Sterne was interred at a new burial ground near Tyburn. As we know, the body was not allowed to rest in peace.

XVII. Sterne's Reputation

As we have seen, when the papers containing the *Journal to Eliza* were deposited with William Makespeace Thackeray in 1851 he did not quote from the unpublished *Journal* in his *English Humorists of the Eighteenth Century*; but the impression of Sterne in his last days that he got from the *Journal* seems only to have fed his pre-existing dislike and disapproval of the author. Thackeray admits that parts of Sterne have charm, but he disapproves of what he sees as the immorality of both the man's life and his works. In the *English Humorists*, he calls Sterne a coward, a blasphemer, wicked, false, a quack, a blubberer, a 'wretched worn-out old scamp', cold-blooded, a mountebank, a 'feeble wretch'; and a purveyor of 'dreary' double-entendres.

Thackeray also attacks Sterne's whole approach to writing, taking exception to his sentimentality and his tendency to try to strike up a personal relationship with the reader. 'He is always looking in my face,' Thackeray complains, 'watching his effect, uncertain whether I think him an impostor or not; posture-making, coaxing, and imploring me'. Sterne 'never lets his reader alone, or will permit his audience repose; when you are quiet, he fancies, he must rouse you, and turns over head and heels, or sidles up and whispers a nasty story'. According to Thackeray, the author of *Tristram Shandy* also stole from other authors and 'put down the theft to the credit side of his own reputation for ingenuity and learning'.

The 'charge of plagiarism', as Traill called it, is not likely to bother modern readers who live in a world where collage and the use of 'found objects' are respected strategies for artists, and where an author like Jonathan Safran Foer can publish his *Tree of Codes* (2010) which is a cut-up version of a novel called *The Street of Crocodiles* by Bruno Schultz (1934). (Readers will notice that the title *Tree of Codes* is a cut-down version of *The Street of Crocodiles*.)

Among the pioneers of collage and the artistic use of found objects in the twentieth century were the Dadaists, a group that included Tristan (not Tristram) Tzara, André Breton and Marcel Duchamp. They experimented with typography and delighted in juxtaposing text and images in unexpected ways: some have seen the black, marbled and blank pages in *Tristram Shandy*, and the book's use of squiggly lines, as precursors of the Dada spirit.

A precursor of Safran Foer's cut-up book can be found in the work of the British artist Tom Phillips. His *A Humument* is a version of a forgotten Victorian novel called *A Human Monument*, which Phillips has transformed by painting over and otherwise obscuring much of the text. It is no coincidence that the front cover of the new Norton Critical edition of *Tristram Shandy* features a page from *A Humument*. In 2016 an exhibition based on this work was also staged at Sterne's old parsonage at Coxwold, and at the time of writing a new edition of *Tristram Shandy* with illustrations by Phillips is due to be released. Sterne's re-purposing of earlier literature is another way in which he was far ahead of his times: he was a post-modernist before even modernism existed.

Virginia Woolf is pre-eminent among English novelists of the modernist school, and it is perhaps not surprising that she often wrote about Sterne in her literary criticism. In an essay on *A Sentimental Journey*, published in the second series of her *Common Reader* essays in 1934, Woolf called Sterne a daring innovator, 'more true to life than literature' and a 'forerunner of the moderns' who was 'on far more intimate terms with us today than his great contemporaries the Richardsons and the Fieldings' . For Woolf:

No writing seems to flow more exactly into the very folds and creases of the individual mind, to express its changing moods, to answer its lightest whim and impulse, and yet the result is perfectly precise and composed. The utmost fluidity exists with the utmost permanence. It is as if the tide raced over the beach hither and thither and left every ripple and eddy cut on the sand in marble.

As a member of a generation that radically re-evaluated Victorian values, Woolf found Thackeray's disapproving attitude to Sterne 'arrogant' and stated that 'to us at the present time, the arrogance of the Victorian novelist seems at least as culpable as the infidelities of the eighteenth-century parson'.

Woolf asserts that 'there are many passages of . . . pure poetry in Sterne,' and goes on to say that 'one can cut them out and read them apart from the text, and yet – for Sterne was a master of the art of contrast – they lie harmoniously side by side on the printed page'. This 'excerptable' quality was exploited in a book called *The Beauties of Sterne*, subtitled 'including all his pathetic tales, and most distinguished observations on life. Selected for the heart of sensibility', which was published in 1782. This was the version of Sterne that was first encountered by Thomas Gibbs, who discovered the *Journal to Eliza*. The varied, mosaic quality of *Tristram Shandy* in particular is mirrored in William S. Burrough's celebrated 1959 novel *The Naked Lunch*. Here the various sections (called 'routines' by Burroughs himself) are certainly not connected in any conventional or logical way, so that the book has a shattered, jagged feel.

In her essay on *A Sentimental Journey*, Woolf draws attention to the way Sterne adopts a 'daring' 'change in the angle of vision' in that book; something I have likened to the use of extreme close-ups in a film. In the twenty-first century, readers and viewers have become so accustomed to shifting and/or unusual points of view on the page or on screen that many will now barely notice the use of this technique. Quentin Tarantino's acclaimed 1994 film *Pulp Fiction* jumps around between different narrative threads and, like Sterne in places, seems to tell the story in the wrong order, or tells the same story from different points of view. Turning again to the works of the American author Jonathan Safran Foer, his 2002 novel *Everything is Illuminated* also switches between different narrative threads and points of view. *Everything is Illuminated* also resembles Sterne's *Sentimental Journey* in that it is in part the story of a journey, and is a novel partly based on a real journey the author made, in this case to Ukraine, the home of his Jewish ancestors.

One of the surprises waiting for the unwary reader in *Tristram Shandy* is the fact that much of the novel is narrated from the point of view of an unborn child. As Ross points out, this is echoed in *Epitaph of a Small Winner* (sometimes translated as *The Posthumous Memoirs of Bras Cubas*), an 1880 novel by the Brazilian Joaquim Maria Machado de Assis, which is supposedly written by a dead man. A better-known novel, written from the point of view of a dead child, is Alice Sebold's *The Lovely Bones* (2002). Ian McEwan's 2016 novel *Nutshell* is told from the point of view of an unborn child, and, like *Tristram Shandy*, has Shakespearian elements, being a modern re-telling of the story of *Hamlet*.

Thackeray complained about Sterne's tendency to remind the reader of his, the author's, existence. 'He is always looking in my face . . . watching his effect'. This approach has the effect of continually reminding readers that they are reading a book – they are not allowed to get 'swept away' by the narrative, and, unlike readers of several of the novels of Daniel Defoe, who died when Sterne was a toddler, readers of Sterne will seldom get the feeling that they are reading a faithful account of real events.

This 'distancing' technique of Sterne's, which Thackeray evidently found too intrusive, resembles the *Verfremdungseffekt* or 'alienation effect' employed by the German playwright Bertolt Brecht (1898-1956). Brecht certainly did not want his audiences to be caught up in or carried away by the action on stage, and he eschewed the popular proscenium-arch or picture-box theatres, which gave audiences the impression that they were gazing through an invisible 'fourth wall' at something real. Brecht's characters talk directly to the audience: he used little in the way of sets or props, and changes of scene would be marked by the appearance of placards stating where the action had now moved.

The idea was to keep audiences awake, to engage their brains and not their hearts.

Similar techniques were employed in the 2005 British film of *Tristram Shandy*, directed by Michael Winterbottom. Titled *A Cock and Bull Story*, at least for its UK release, the film switches between re-enactments of events described in Sterne's novel and faux-documentary behind-the-scenes footage of the actors and crew actually making the film. The serious problems that confront the film-makers reflect the sense in *Tristram Shandy* that the narrator is struggling to keep his narrative afloat, and that he is sometimes forced to improvise to make things work. As the volumes of his novel were released, Sterne was also acutely aware of what the critics had already said, and what they were likely to say in response to his later volumes. In *A Cock and Bull Story*, the actors playing the director and producer of the film are similarly concerned, and are shown trying to cope with various problems and mistakes that have to be tackled during production. Tony Wilson, a real-life TV arts presenter, appears in the film, where he interviews the leading actor. There is also a reference to Tristram's mysterious mistress, Jenny. In the film, the lead actor's wife and his mistress are called Jenny and Jennie, respectively.

As we have seen, Sterne's books tend to blend into each other and into his real life, refusing to be self-contained. This is the case with the *Cock and Bull* film, which, in its DVD incarnation, has special features including extended versions of scenes and a chatty tour of Sterne's old parsonage at Coxwold. The chattee on this tour is the English actor and writer Stephen Fry, who also plays Parson Yorick and a fictitious curator of the Coxwold parsonage, in the film. The bantering relationship between the two leading actors, Rob Brydon and Steve Coogan, as depicted in the film, has since metamorphosed into a series of humorous travel documentaries featuring the pair.

Although there is to date only one film version of *Tristram Shandy*, there have been radio adaptations over the years, and in 1996 the British cartoonist and writer Martin Rowson produced a large-format black and white cartoon book of *Tristram Shandy*, following this up with a version of *A Sentimental Journey* in 2018.

Rowson's *Tristram* is dark and disturbing. Practically every person depicted is ugly, and, as happens in parts of the works of one of Sterne's inspirations, François Rabelais, the more ridiculous and repulsive aspects of human anatomy are emphasised and exaggerated. Although Rowson has to squeeze a novel of over four hundred pages into under two hundred pages, and still find room for his pictures, the artist includes extra characters, dialogue and analysis. He also includes illustrations based on his idea of how famous artists like Aubrey Beardsley and Albrecht Dürer might have illustrated *Tristram*.

Some of the earliest prints and illustrations based on Sterne's *Tristram Shandy*, particularly those by Henry Bunbury (1750-1811) are as deliberately crude and distorted as those to be found in Rowson's version. A more decorous idea of Sterne can be found in pictures like Angelika Kaufmann's painting of Maria of Moulines, who appears in both *Tristram* and the *Journey*.

Kauffmann's painting was transformed into an engraving and reproduced on various household items such as watch-cases and tables. This was an early version of the ubiquitous modern practice of 'merchandising': the inclusion of licensed images and other content on everything from t-shirts to children's lunch-boxes. Something similar happened following the first publication of the novel *Werther* in 1774. All over Europe, young men took to wearing yellow waistcoats like Goethe's eponymous hero, and there were Werther tea-sets and even a perfume. From the 1780s the celebrated English potter Josiah Wedgwood produced jasperware pieces inspired by Sterne's works – these were designed by the artist Elizabeth, Lady Templetown (1746-1823). Wedgwood also made busts and cameo reliefs of the writer.

Current Sterne merchandise includes *Tristram*'s missing Chapter XXIV, now finally written by the American poet Craig Dworkin. Dworkin follows in the footsteps of Sterne's friend John Hall-Stevenson, who asserted that *A Sentimental Journey* was left unfinished at Sterne's death: Hall-Stevenson published a continuation, together with a short memoir of his friend and an edition of *A Political Romance*. In his *Continuation*, Hall-Stevenson (or whoever wrote the book) shows himself to be as reluctant as Sterne himself to take his hero Yorick to Italy, and opts to keep him in Paris for most of the action. Here the clergyman renews his acquaintance with a charming Parisian glove-seller, and various other characters from *A Sentimental Journey*. Hall-Stevenson's version of Yorick seeks out Maria of Moulines, but finds only her freshly-dug grave. Hall-Stevenson then returns Yorick (not altogether safely) to England. Before either Dworkin or Hall-Stevenson, one John Carr published a spurious Volume III of *Tristram Shandy* in 1760.

Various CDs and audio downloads, prints, and issues of the scholarly Sterne journal, *The Shandean,* fill out the Sterne merchandising offer. In the same way that devotees of Mickey Mouse simply must visit a Disney theme-park, lovers of Sterne must make the pilgrimage to Shandy Hall, the master's old parsonage at Coxwold.

It may seem fanciful to call Sterne's old parsonage a 'hall', but in fact this particular Yorkshire parsonage was originally built as a medieval long hall, in the early fifteenth century. Visitors combining a trip to Shandy Hall with a visit to the nearby city of York can get an idea of what the hall at Coxwold might have looked like in medieval times by seeking out Barley Hall in York's Coffee Yard. The Laurence Sterne Trust acquired Shandy Hall in 1968, and it now houses an internationally important collection of Sterne-related books, manuscripts, paintings, prints and other items.

Select Bibliography

Anonymous: *Aristotle's Masterpiece*, L. René, 1800

Burroughs, William S.: *Naked Lunch*, Penguin, 2015

Burton, John: *A Letter to William Smellie*, 1753

Burton, John: *A Treatise on the Non-Naturals*, A. Staples, 1738

Burton, Robert: *Anatomy of Melancholy*, Penguin, 2020

Carpenter, S.C.: *Eighteenth Century Church and People*, John Murray, 1959

Childs, John: *The British Army of William III*, Manchester University Press, 1987

Davies, Robert: *A Memoir of the York Press*, Nichols & Sons, 1868

Dickens, Charles: *Great Expectations*, Pan, 1974

Diderot, Denis: *Jacques the Fatalist*, Oxford, 2008

Diderot, Denis: *The Nun*, Oxford, 2008

Ferriar, John: *Illustrations of Sterne, &c.*, Cadell and Davies, 1798

Fielding, Henry: *Joseph Andrews and Shamela*, Oxford, 2008

Foer, Jonathan Safran: *Everything is Illuminated*, Penguin, 2003

Foer, Jonathan Safran: *Tree of Codes*, Visual Editions, 2010

Gray, Thomas and Collins, William: *Gray & Collins Poetical Works*, Oxford, 1937

Gwynne, Stephen: *The History of Ireland*, Macmillan, 1924

Hall-Stevenson, John: *Works*, Debrett, Beckett, 1795

Hall-Stevenson, John: *Yorick's Sentimental Journey Continued*, Georgian Society, 1902

Hewins, W.A.S.: *The Whitefoord Papers*, Oxford, 1898

Hogarth, William: *The Analysis of Beauty*, Yale, 1997

Homer (trans. A. Pope): *The Iliad and Odyssey*, Routledge, 1890

Hyde, Douglas: *A Literary History of Ireland*, T. Fisher Unwin, 1899

Johnson, Samuel: *Rasselas*, Oxford, 2009

Locke, John: *An Essay Concerning Human Understanding*, Eliz. Holt, 1690

Macdonald, John: *Memoirs of an Eighteenth Century Footman*, Routledge, 2004

Machado de Assis, Joaquim Maria: *The Posthumous Memoirs of Brás Cubas*, Penguin, 2020

McEwan, Ian: *Nutshell*, Vintage, 2017

Pinger, W.R.R.: *Laurence Sterne and Goethe*, University of California, 1920

Plumb, J.H.: *England in the Eighteenth Century*, Penguin, 1950

Pope, Alexander: *Poems*, Routledge, 1966

Prior, James: *Life of Edmond Malone*, Smith, Elder & Co., 1860

Richter, Hans: *Dada*, Thames & Hudson, 1965

Ross, Ian Campbell: *Laurence Sterne: A Life*, Oxford, 2001

Rowson, Martin: *Tristram Shandy*, Selfmadehero, 2010

Sancho, Ignatius: *Letters of the Late Ignatius Sancho*, Penguin, 1998

Sebold, Alice: *The Lovely Bones*, Picador, 2003

Shakespeare, William: *Hamlet*, Oxford, 2008

Sheridan, R.B.: *The School for Scandal*, Oxford, 2008

Smollett, Tobias: *Peregrine Pickle*, Oxford, 1969

Smollett, Tobias: *Travels Through France and Italy*, Oxford, 1707

Sterne, Laurence: *The Journal to Eliza and Various Letters*, J.F. Taylor & Co., 1904

Sterne, Laurence: *The Life and Opinions of Tristram Shandy, Gent*, Everyman, 1915

Sterne, Laurence: *A Political Romance*, Club of Odd Volumes, 1914

Sterne, Laurence: *A Sentimental Journey and Other Writings*, Oxford, 2003

Sterne, Laurence: *A Sentimental Journey and the Journal to Eliza*, Everyman, 1926

Sterne, Laurence: *Tristram Shandy*, Norton, 2019

Swift, Jonathan: *Gulliver's Travels*, Norton, 2002

Swift, Jonathan: *A Modest Proposal and Other Writings*, Penguin, 2009

Thackeray, W.M.: *English Humorists of the Eighteenth Century*, Scott, Foresman & Co., 1911

Traill, H.D.: *Sterne*, Harper, 1901

Virgil (trans. John Dryden): *Aeneid*, Penguin, 1997

Virgil: *The Eclogues and Georgics*, Oxford, 2009

Walpole, Horace: *The Castle of Otranto*, Oxford, 2014

Whittaker, Ruth: *Tristram Shandy*, Open University Press, 1988

Wolf, Tom: *The Pump House Gang*, Black Swan, 1989

Woolf, Virginia: *The Common Reader, Volume 2*, Vintage, 2003

For free downloads and more from the Langley Press,
please visit our website at http://tinyurl.com/lpdirect